how2become.com

How to Write & Publish a Bestselling Book

My journey from firefighter to bestselling author, and how you can do it too!

By Richard McMunn

- "I reinvented myself as a bestselling writer"
- "I learned how to publish books AND keep all the profits"
- "I can teach YOU the secrets of my success"

Orders: Please contact How2Become Ltd, Suite 1, 60 Churchill Square Business Centre, Kings Hill, Kent ME19 4YU. You can also order via the email address info@How2Become.co.uk.

ISBN: 9781912370115

First published in 2019 by How2Become Ltd

Typeset for How2Become Ltd by Gemma Butler.

Printed in Great Britain for How2Become Ltd by CMP.

AS PART OF THIS BOOK I WANT YOU TO DOWNLOAD A FREE AUTHOR TOOLKIT – WITHIN THIS TOOLKIT I HAVE SUPPLIED YOU WITH SOME USEFUL TRAINING VIDEOS, A BOOK WRITING TEMPLATE AND THE EXACT ACTION PLAN I HAVE BEEN USING FOR THE LAST FEW YEARS THAT HAS ENABLED ME TO BECOME A BESTSELLING AUTHOR AND AWARD-WINNING PUBLISHER.

YOU CAN DOWNLOAD THE TOOLKIT AT:

WWW.AUTHORTOOLKIT.CO.UK

"You need no qualifications or prior experience to write and self-publish a book. All you need is an idea, hard work, determination and a willingness to learn."

"Write a book that oozes quality. When writing your book, focus on the reader and how it will benefit them. Do not focus on how much money the book will make for you."

"Your cover design is absolutely crucial to your book's overall success. It does not matter how good your content is, if the book cover design is poor, you will sell few copies."

"When writing your book, think about the different opportunities to upsell or connect with your readers."

"Write a minimum of 3 pages every day. After a month, you'll have almost 100 pages of content."

"Have a mentor to help navigate your way through the writing and publishing process – you'll achieve your goals much faster!"

Richard McMunn

Award-winning publisher and bestselling author

WELCOME

Dear author,

It gives me tremendous pleasure to bring you this book, which is a collaboration of many years of hard work, determination and a willingness to learn.

As you read this book you will notice that in order to write and self-publish a book you need no prior experience of the publishing world. This might seem surprising, but it's actually really simple! What you *do* need is a willingness to learn, and a mentor (someone who will help you).

To make this book as interesting and inspiring as possible I've included sections on my own life story. I have written from the heart, sharing key details about my background and my personal journey and, most importantly, spelling out the lessons that I have learned along the way.

I must stress that the methods that I am going to teach you within the book are not the only way to get your book finished and published – they are simply the methods that I have tried and tested, and the ones that have worked for me. You will also notice that I urge you not to go out and get a book publishing deal with a major or independent publisher. The reason for this is simply because I believe the effort it takes to get a book publishing deal can be better channelled into doing it yourself. If you follow the steps and guidance I have provided within this book, you will be able to do it yourself. In many cases I believe you will probably do a better job than some of the established publishing houses that are out there!

You will notice the book has been divided up into 3 separate sections for ease of reading. SECTIONS ONE and THREE are about my inspirational journey from how I left school with poor grade GCSEs but still managed to achieve great success as an author and award-winning publisher. If you have no interest in my backstory (including the lessons learnt along the way) and you simply want to understand the steps it takes to write and publish a bestselling book, feel free to jump straight to SECTION TWO of the book.

Finally, after reading my book, please utilise the free author toolkit I have provided you with. It contains several useful training videos and resources to help your journey to becoming a bestselling author. To access the free toolkit, please go to:

www.AuthorToolkit.co.uk

To your success,

Richard McMunn

P.S. I strongly believe success is a choice. If you want to write and publish a bestselling book, you CAN do it! Always work hard, learn as you go and maintain a positive mind-set and attitude.

Acknowledgments

Thanks to my mum for her love and support over the years. You've always been there for me through thick and thin.

To my daughter for being who you are! I'm very proud of you.

Rachel Murphy for her time, patience and expert help in putting this book together.

Everyone at How2Become.com for making our business great and for your continued hard work in striving for the best for our readers.

Joshua Brown for applying for *that* 'admin assistant' role a few years ago – I always knew you'd make Managing Director!

All my friends in the Royal Navy and the Fire Service.

My old Sub Officer (Mick) who took me under his wing when I joined the Fire Service. Although you are not with us anymore, I'll never forget how you helped me and the opportunities you put my way.

To Simon Coulson for being a great business mentor and friend.

Thanks to all the authors who have successfully completed my VIP Author Mentoring Programme. I loved every minute of working with you guys and seeing you reach your writing and publishing goals.

Finally, thanks to you for buying this book. I genuinely hope you find the content both inspiring and informative and that you achieve your own goal of getting your first book published.

Contents

Prologue

'Please step on the weighing scales.'

I was stripped down to my y-fronts, burning with embarrassment and feeling completely out of my comfort zone. The grey-haired doctor had already run a few basic medical checks, including the 'cough and drop' test. Having the elderly doctor touch me 'there' was the weirdest experience of my life. I was mortified.

I was just 16 years old and, to be honest, I'd got myself into this situation by being lazy and undisciplined. I'd dropped the ball in a big way at school, and GCSE results day had been a shocker. I scraped together just three passes, and to say my dad was disappointed is something of an understatement.

'There's only one thing for it, son,' he declared. 'You'll have to join the Royal Navy.'

'The Royal Navy? Will I?'

'Yes, you will. The Navy it is. What else are you going to do with three GCSEs?'

I had no answer to that. I'd always imagined I'd follow in Dad's footsteps and join the fire brigade, but you couldn't do that until you were 18 years old. It looked like I had no other option but to do as my father was telling me.

The following week Dad escorted me from our home in Leyland to the Armed Forces careers office in Preston.

'My lad wants to join the Royal Navy,' he confidently informed the Warrant Officer.

'No I don't,' I thought to myself.

I looked at Dad. He had done very well for himself, rising quickly through the ranks in the Lancashire Fire Service. He was proudly dressed in his Assistant Divisional Officer's uniform, while I was in a snug-fitting suit and a flowery tie he'd picked out for me. Before we left home, Dad had checked my shoes were shining and had even cleaned my ears, though when I look back I can see that nothing he did that day could have stopped me from being wet behind the ears!

The Warrant Officer looked like Uncle Albert from *Only Fools and Horses,* though he was ruthlessly efficient. He started filling out forms there and then. Dad was smiling his approval and, in the blink of an eye, I found myself signing my application form to join the Royal Navy. It was that fast, that simple.

I passed the selection exams with ease and, almost before I could catch my breath, I was being asked which division of the Navy I was interested in.

'I like aircraft,' I said, thinking of all the Airfix model planes I'd made as a young boy.

'Would you like to fix aircraft?'

'Er, yes. I would.'

I was told I could train as an Air Engineering Mechanic (AEM) and I liked the sound of that. In fact, by this stage joining the Navy was actually starting to appeal to me. Now all I needed to do was re-sit my Maths GCSE and get a pass grade, then have a routine medical examination. Then I'd be off the join the Navy! How easy was this?

I signed up at our local sixth form college to do the maths re-sit and felt very proud of myself when I told the other kids I was joining the Navy in a few months' time. They were extremely impressed, and I loved the reaction I got.

'The Navy? Wow! That's cool. Will you get to go round the world?'

'Yes,' I beamed, though I didn't have a clue which countries I might go to, or when.

All I knew was that joining the Navy did sound like a very cool thing to do, and it certainly beat staying on at school or college. I was beginning to really put my shoulders back and feel excited about my new life and career. I was incredibly nervous too about what lay ahead, but I was definitely up for the challenge.

I had no worries about passing my Maths GCSE; I was capable, but I'd simply not put any effort into the exam last time round. The medical didn't faze me either. I was six foot tall and was a strong, strapping lad with no injuries or health problems. I was going to pass with flying colours and then I'd be signing my papers to join the Navy in no time at all, just as I'd told everyone I would.

'Please step on the weighing scales.'

I'll never forget the doctor saying those words to me. As I stepped onto the old-fashioned scales I heard the cogs groaning under my weight. Looking down I saw the needle lurching with alarming speed to the right. I'd never weighed myself before and I had no idea how heavy I was. To my horror the needle smashed through the 13 and then the 14 stone mark, before giving a little quiver and finally resting at 15 stone. I was shocked, to say the least. Was 15 stone really how much I weighed?

'Oh dear,' the doctor said, peering at the scales over the edge of his spectacles. He looked extremely unimpressed.

I gulped and got dressed silently as the doctor filled in my medical assessment form.

'I'm afraid you've failed,' he said, unnecessarily. 'You need to lose a stone in weight before you can start your Navy training course.'

I gulped again. Then the doctor gave me a diet sheet and meal planner and sent me on my way. I felt utterly dejected as I walked to the bus stop on Garstang Road in Preston, staring at the details of the miserable diet I was expected to go on. I could never survive on rabbit food like that, or such tiny portions!

I wanted to cry. How could I tell everyone I was too fat to join the Royal Navy? This was utterly devastating. My Navy career was over before it had even begun and, more importantly, what the hell was I going to do now?

I didn't realise it at the time, but I was about to make a decision that would change the course of my life. When the bus pulled up I didn't get on it. I decided to walk home instead, at a brisk pace and with an increasing feeling of hope in my heart as my blood began to pump faster around my body. I could do this, I started to think. I could lose the weight. And if I put my mind to it and worked hard I could do it quickly, so nobody need know about this blip. All I needed was to be determined and disciplined. I'd lose the weight before I even left college. Of course I could do it!

On my walk home I told myself over and over again I was going to succeed. There was no question about it, because what was the alternative? I had no Plan B and therefore I had to make Plan A work.

I can see now that that day signalled the beginning of my journey to career success. Today, I still remember my 16-year-old self every time I'm faced with a new challenge, in any area of my life. However huge the task ahead I know I have a choice, and that my future is in my own hands. I ask myself, do I want to stand still or be carried through life, or am I prepared to work hard, be proactive and make my next dream come true? The answer is *always* the latter.

This attitude has enabled me to reinvent myself as a prolific writer and bestselling published author. I've proven repeatedly that when I'm determined and disciplined and prepared to work hard I will write my book, publish it and profit from it. I've written well over a hundred books to date, a vast number of them Amazon bestsellers, so I know my methods work!

Throughout my life I've learned many more important lessons that have helped me become a bestselling author, as well as an award-winning publisher. I sincerely hope that by sharing my life story as well as my insider knowledge I can help YOU follow your dream and become a happy published author too.

WRITE 3 PAGES OF CONTENT A DAY... AFTER A MONTH, YOU'LL HAVE ALMOST 100 PAGES!

Richard McMunn

SECTION ONE – MY STORY
CHAPTER 1 -
The Early Years

'Do you want your car washing?'

I was standing on the drive of our neighbour's house, admiring his impressive sports car. Marcel had a Porsche 911 with blue leather seats and a white fin on the back. It was totally awesome and I didn't think for one minute he was going to let me anywhere near it. I'd fill up my water buckets at home and walk all over our estate in Leyland, knocking on doors to drum up customers.

I called my business **Rick's Mobile Car Wash and Valeting Service**, and I worked tirelessly every Saturday and Sunday, starting really early in the morning.

Marcel looked me up and down.

'Yes,' he said. 'You can wash my car.'

My jaw dropped and then I grinned from ear to ear. I'd have paid *him* to be allowed to clean his car, never mind the other way around!

I took great care as I washed the Porsche, and from that day on Marcel became one of my many regular customers. I can vividly remember washing Marcel's Porsche and thinking to myself – 'I'm going to get my own Porsche one day!'

I was a spotty 15-year-old, charging £2 a time for a car wash. I usually made about £50 a day from my little enterprise, and I was doing so well that when I was still 15 I even started to wonder if I should try to expand and turn this into a proper, grown-up business when I left school.

Becoming a firefighter like Dad was the only other idea I had for a future career, and I guess that was hardly surprising. I'd watched my dad's career in the Fire Service flourish throughout my childhood. He was devoted to his job, very good at it, and he rose through the ranks with apparent ease and he seemed proud and very happy in his work.

There was a price to pay for Dad's success, however. When I was 12 years old he was offered a three-year secondment in the Cotswolds. By this time I'd already attended a couple of different primary schools as Dad was promoted into various posts around Lancashire, and I'd just started at secondary school in Leyland.

'We're moving to Moreton-in-Marsh,' he announced.

'Moreton-in-what? Where's that?'

'The Cotswolds.'

'Oh.'

I'd never been there and I didn't want to go. I was just three months into my first year at secondary school, I had my group of mates and I didn't want to be uprooted to another part of the country and be the new kid with the northern accent.

Mum was very loving and supportive and she listened to my concerns. My sister was a year ahead at school and arguably in an even worse predicament than me, so this was not easy for any of us. Our parents understood our reservations, but ultimately we had to accept that Dad's career came first. The fact was, he was the main breadwinner in the family and this was an amazing opportunity for him, so we had no choice but to bite the bullet and get on with it.

Mum explained that we'd live in the beautiful Gloucestershire countryside for three years, and then the likelihood was we would return to Lancashire when I was 15. I'd then be able to return to my old school to finish my secondary education. My parents tried to make the move sound as appealing as possible, but I knew this definitely wasn't going to be good. I was going to spend my early teenage years feeling like a fish out of water, and by the time we got back to Lancashire – if we ever did – I'd be slap bang in the middle of my GCSE year. What's more, I'd have missed out on three years' of friendship with my old mates and I'd most probably be viewed as the new boy all over again. This could only be terrible news and I was very pessimistic, but what choice did I have? The decision was made and I was going to have to pack my bags, say my goodbyes and make the best of my new life in the Cotswolds.

My journey to my new school, Chipping Campden High School, was terrible. I had to sit on a coach for an hour and I didn't even want to reach my destination, not ever! I hated Moreton-in-Marsh and I hated Chipping Campden High School.

I can't remember the lessons but I have some very clear recollections of a chain of events that happened not too long after I arrived. In the first memory I'm crying in the classroom, then I'm being bullied and then SMACK! I had decked another pupil. After that I was suspended for a few days and my mum and dad went absolutely mental. I had no desire to return to the classroom after my suspension but, once again, I had no choice in the matter. I had to do as I was told.

I coasted through school, counting the months, weeks and finally the days until we returned to Lancashire. There was only one really good thing I recall from my time at Chipping Campden High School. I liked acting, and I thoroughly enjoyed myself when I took part in the school production of *Bugsy Malone*. I didn't have a big part but I loved performing, and I thought it was great when the local paper ran a story about the show and printed some photos of all the cast. We raised money for the Ethiopian Famine Relief Fund to boot, which made the whole event really worthwhile.

Putting on a show was infinitely more interesting than anything that might happen inside a classroom. When I was younger I'd also put myself forward to be Joseph in the Christmas Nativity and this ended up in the local paper too. I looked a right idiot in my dressing gown, but I still enjoyed the overall experience. I was comfortable in the limelight, but I never considered acting might be something I could do as a future career: Drama was just an enjoyable distraction from the tedium of academic lessons.

It was drummed into me at school that I had to do well in my exams in order to make something of myself. It wasn't what I wanted to hear because I was not a natural student, but I accepted this was the way of the world. I knew that if I wanted to do my dad proud and join the Fire Service like him one day I'd need to have some decent qualifications under my belt, but I still found it a struggle to concentrate and knuckle down. My attention span was very short but that was just another thing I had to cope with as best I could.

It was 1985 when I finally re-joined my old school in Lancashire, Balshaw's High School. Mobile phones and social media didn't exist back then of course, and so I hadn't spoken to my mates for the entire three years I'd been away. Some of the lads had changed beyond all recognition, and my return wasn't smooth.

'Mick wants to fight you,' I was told on the school field one day.

Mick was cock of the school, and it seemed he'd taken one look at me and decided I needed to be shown who was boss. I was already six foot and must have been tipping the scales at 15 stone even then, and I assume this Mick character thought I was some kind of threat to him. In fact I was anything but. I was the strong and sensitive type, and I wanted nothing but a quiet transition back into my old life after my years of unrest and unhappiness in the Cotswolds.

Mick and I had a massive fight that culminated in me pinning him down and punching him. Then I pulled myself up and ran off, because I didn't even want to be there in the first place!

Academically I was being pushed to punch above my weight, which was a pressure. Balshaw's had previously been a grammar school and the standards were higher than I was used to. Having put very little effort into my lessons over the past three years I had a lot of catching up to do in the classroom, but unfortunately I had precious little time left to get myself up to speed for my GCSEs. I think a part of me had given up before I reached the end. I'd left it too late, I was lazy and I was lacking in motivation. My secondary school life had been seriously disrupted, so what was the point in even trying?

A slim, frizzy-haired English teacher called Frieda was the only member of staff who really inspired me. I liked all of her literature and language lessons and I think she recognised that she lit a spark in me, because she persevered with me even when I wasn't putting in as much effort as I should. I was still quite lazy, even in English, but at least I was engaged with the lessons and, thanks to Frieda, I wanted to learn.

Art was the only other subject I was interested in. The school asked me to create a mural for the wall which I thoroughly enjoyed doing and was proud of when I saw it on display. I loved being creative and looked forward to every art lesson, although at that age I hadn't yet recognised how important it was to *feed* my creativity.

Dancing and music were my other passions. I got into breakdancing and loved it, and when a chance came up for me to play the drums at weekends I grabbed it with both hands. This opportunity presented itself when my sister started to go out with a boy called Phil who lived at the top of our road. Our parents would only allow my sister to go round to her boyfriend's house if I went with her, so we came to an arrangement that suited us all. This was the deal: I was allowed to play on Phil's sparkly silver drum kit while my sister and her boyfriend got an hour to themselves on Sunday afternoons. What a result! I loved drumming and I taught myself to play in just ten weeks. I really wanted a drum kit of my own but we couldn't afford it, so I always made the most of every minute I had to play at Phil's house.

I started going to music lessons at school and I formed a band with a few other kids. We called ourselves Sound Advice and the music teacher allowed us to put on a concert to raise money for charity. I already fancied the music teacher before she let us do this, and now I was her number one fan! Without giving it a second thought I put myself forward as the project manager and the concert was a great success. There was just one small issue. All the money we raised was spent on hiring the instruments, and so it wasn't really the charity fundraiser it set out to be! Nonetheless it was a fantastic experience and I felt very pleased with what we achieved. I loved the buzz of being up on stage and seeing everything coming together after all our hard work.

In hindsight, project managing and performing came very naturally to me, but at that age I didn't analyse my characteristics or consider that I should look for a job that used those skills. I was still too young to think like that and besides, in my mind, I was probably always going to end up joining the Fire Service like Dad. This was something I'd imagined from such a young age, without ever really questioning whether the job would suit me or ultimately make me feel happy and fulfilled at work. It was almost an inevitable path I felt I'd been on throughout my childhood, even though neither of my parents or any of my teachers ever told me this was what I should do, and I hadn't taken any steps towards making this happen.

When the GCSE results came in it was time to take a long, hard look at my life. I can vividly remember going to school to collect my grades. Other kids were hugging and crying and laughing with relief but when I opened my envelope I just stood there in shock. I stared at my three pass grades. I hadn't worked hard, but even so I'd expected to do better than this! I had just two measly Cs in English Language and English Literature and a B in Art. This latter grade was only thanks to the fact my art teacher had really looked after me, and the mural I made for the school wall was submitted as part of my course work.

Maybe I could expand my mobile car wash round? That's a good idea! Perhaps I could turn it into a proper business?

That was one of the many thoughts that went through my head as I tried to digest my extremely disappointing exam results. I really had not expected to do so badly. I'd anticipated going on to do A levels or having my pick of college courses or even jobs. I'd imagined I'd be taking more exams or gaining some useful qualifications over the next two years before potentially joining the Fire Service at 18, which was the earliest entry age. Now I had no idea what I was going to do. Who was going to take me on with these GCSE grades? I would have to expand my car wash business, wouldn't I? That was it. That was what I was going to do!

As I've already described, Dad had a very different idea.

'The Navy it is. What else are you going to do with three GCSEs?'

I didn't waste my breath by discussing my car wash expansion idea. Dad was on a mission, and I was already on my way to sign the papers.

LESSONS LEARNED FROM MY EARLY YEARS

If you don't ask you don't get. I asked Marcel if I could wash his Porsche even when I expected to be turned down flat. There is nothing to lose from being optimistic and proactive, and there could be a lot to gain. Be polite and courteous, and ask away! Knowledge is never wasted and will inform your writing.

Take pride in every job you do. I washed every car with great care, no matter what make or model it was, or what condition it was in. Customers are king. Be proud of your work and never forget that it is your job to meet the needs and expectations of your customers and readers.

Keep a positive attitude. We all experience negative situations in our lives, but it's how we respond to them that's important. If you feel stuck in a rut, talk it through or seek help and advice from a mentor instead of complaining and rebelling. A negative attitude will spill on to the page and will hamper your writing and publishing ventures. Writing a book is a new and fresh opportunity for you, so make the most of it by being focused, positive and disciplined.

Never say 'I can't do it!'. I am a strong believer you can achieve whatever you want in life. Many a time I have heard aspiring authors say they don't feel they have the confidence to write or publish a book, and that they are afraid of failure. The truth is, if you do nothing, you get nothing. There is no risk whatsoever in writing your book. Just sit down and start writing!

Recognise what makes you tick. At school I loved Art, English, Music and Drama, but I didn't realise I needed to do something *creative* with my life! If you're reading this you've probably already recognised you are a creative person. Now, think about what makes your creativity flow. Being inspired by the topic you are writing about will boost your productivity and success as an author.

SELF-PUBLISHING GIVES YOU 100% OF THE ROYALTIES, AND TOTAL CONTROL OVER EVERYTHING.

Richard McMunn

CHAPTER 2 -
Joining the Navy

I studied the diet sheet the doctor had given me when I failed my Navy medical after leaving school, and this is what it said:

Breakfast - scrambled eggs on two slices of toast with one cup of tea.

Mid-morning snack – one apple

Lunch – one jacket potato with small portion of beans

Afternoon snack – one banana

Evening meal – one small portion of chicken breast, half a cup of boiled rice and vegetables

Evening snack – one wholemeal biscuit and a small glass of milk

(Note – drink one pint of water 20 minutes before each meal)

It was probably half of what I normally ate, which explains why I was overweight. I'd never stopped to consider the number of calories I was putting into my body or, more importantly, whether I was burning up enough of them every day. I often made myself a snack of double egg on toast at 9pm and never thought twice about it.

Things were going to have to change. I'd already made that decision when I walked home from the doctor's instead of getting the bus. I knew that the only way I could avoid the humiliation of telling my friends I was too fat to join the Navy was by *not* being too fat to join the Navy. I was going to lose my excess stone in weight and I was going to do it as quickly as I safely could.

At the time I had a fantastic and supportive girlfriend called Lisa, and I'd loved her reaction when I first told her I was joining the Navy. She was very impressed, and I thought about Lisa when I worked out what I had to do to pass my medical. I didn't want to disappoint Lisa and I certainly didn't want her to look at me as a failure. My GCSE results had been enough of a choker: I was not going to fall down again.

I couldn't avoid telling my parents I'd failed the medical and I was dreading telling them the news, but their reaction was great. Mum was typically supportive, and Dad instantly offered to help. Dad was always a great problem solver, which is what you'd expect from him being in the Fire Service, and he was about to teach me a valuable lesson in being disciplined.

'You're coming running with me,' he said. 'We'll do three miles at 6am every morning before you go to college.'

'OK,' I agreed. 'I can do that.'

It was September and I wanted to lose the weight by the time I'd done my maths re-sit in January. Then there would be no delay and I'd be all ready to join the Navy exactly as I'd planned, and without having to reveal my shame to my mates.

When my alarm clock rang at the crack of dawn every morning I reminded myself of this fact and got out of bed straight away. I had no choice. There was no room for laziness or I'd fail my medical once again. Having both my parents supporting me was a huge help. I didn't want to let either of them down, and they encouraged me every day.

It wasn't as difficult as I feared it would be to stick to the diet. I'd got into bad habits that I hadn't even recognised until now, but once I was aware of what I had to do I didn't find it hard to re-train myself. Again, thinking about the consequences of *not* losing the weight spurred me on. I asked myself, 'What is the point of running three miles at 6am every morning if I'm not going to change my eating habits? Why overeat if it means my reputation with my mates and my girlfriend is on the line? What will I do with my life if I don't get in the Navy?'

I can see now that the fact I was just 16 years old helped me a great deal. Not only did I have the support of my parents at home to keep me on track with my exercise and diet, but I had a naïve view on life that gave me a massive incentive too. My immaturity and lack of life experience meant I believed my whole world would come crashing in if I didn't lose the weight. It would have done, for a short time, but back then I imagined I'd be doomed forever if I failed to jump this one hurdle!

I lost a stone in just four weeks, and the next time I stepped off the same set of weighing scales at the doctor's surgery I felt euphoric instead of horrified. I liked the feeling. It was good to succeed and to see how my hard work had paid off. This time the doctor looked impressed, and I walked out of his surgery feeling pumped up with pride. I didn't even consider taking the bus. My habits and my mindset had changed and I was not going back to my old ways.

I'll never forget the day I left home to join the Navy. It was January 1989 when my family and my girlfriend Lisa waved me off at Preston station as I embarked on a twelve-hour journey to Torpoint in Cornwall. I was training at HMS Raleigh in Plymouth, the famous purpose-built training base where every sailor began his naval career. To help prepare me, I'd been sent a Royal Navy booklet outlining what would happen over the coming weeks.

'Most young men enjoy their time at HMS Raleigh,' it said on the first page. 'We believe that you will too. But in the last resort, this will depend on you: on your determination to succeed, your willingness to take the rough with the smooth, to welcome the experiences cheerfully and to learn from them.'

It was good advice for life in general let alone in the Navy, though once again I was too young to recognise it at the time. As I read the booklet on my train journey south I was more taken with other very important snippets of information, such as the fact there would be steak and kidney pies, Chicken Maryland and Bakewell tart on the menu! I was also very much looking forward to wearing my uniforms and taking part in parades. Imagine that!

Before I had left Preston, and whenever I spoke to my friends back home about the Navy, it all sounded so glamorous. Most of my mates were staying on at school or college or starting jobs locally. My chosen path seemed the most exciting by a long way, but as I travelled further and further from home the scales began to fall from my eyes. This was incredibly daunting. I wondered what I was going to find at the other end of the country. I wouldn't have any friends and I'd miss my mum and dad, my sister and my girlfriend. What had I agreed to?

I gave myself a talking to and I knew there was no point in panicking or trying to turn back. I was going to give this my best shot, because what choice did I have? I'd be miserable and embarrassed if I bottled it and pulled out now. There was no question about it: I was joining the Navy and the next time I came home I'd be holding my head high, I'd have stories to tell and I'd be feeling very good about myself.

My nerves were snapping like elastic bands around my body by the time I arrived at Torpoint. There were loads of other lads like me on the train, and as we disembarked a big bloke dressed in a Royal Navy uniform holding a big stick and a clipboard barked at us.

'Get your hands out of your pockets!'

We were put in transit vans and driven through two large gates into the training centre where we would be spending six weeks doing basic training.

'That's the end of your freedom boys,' we were told as the van entered the gates.

This was starting to feel more like a prison sentence than a fabulous new career. Next I was given a 'number four', having all my hair cut off. Then I was given the task of cleaning a room. I'd never used a Hoover in my life before and this was all too much - I wanted to throw the towel in there and then! It was terrible, and homesickness was seeping through me really badly, making me feel so peculiar and lonely.

I was given my number - D220847G – and in that moment my isolation was complete. I was just a number now. I didn't want to be just a number. I wanted to be back home in Lancashire, eating my tea with my family, knocking about with my friends and just being ME again. How was I going to cope here, all alone? I wasn't alone, of course. There were loads of other young lads in the same boat as me, but we didn't know each other, not yet. We were all given our 'Frank Spencer' berets and at that point there was a sense of us all being in this together. This brought some small comfort, but even so it was tough.

I can remember being in the middle of a crowd of lads with Scottish accents. I couldn't understand what they were saying and afterwards, when I was on my own, I burst into tears, thinking about how much I missed my girlfriend. That night I rang my mum and told her I wanted to go home, and then Dad came on the phone.

'If you quit this, what will you do?'

I had no answer. I knew if I wanted to leave now I could apply for a 'PVR' – a pre-voluntary release. I wanted to leave, but I didn't want the humiliation of dropping out like this, or the problem of what I'd do instead.

'I'll stay,' I told my parents, even though my bottom lip was wobbling as I said those two life-changing words.

I did stick at it, and thankfully life in the Navy did get better. I became very good at ironing and cleaning, as well as polishing my shoes. I started to feel a sense of ownership about my life. My destiny was in my hands. I had a strong sense that I could choose how this was going to go, by choosing how much work to put in.

I worked and trained hard for six solid weeks, doing drills, getting up at 2am to go for a run, cleaning, ironing, and doing everything that was asked of me to the very best of my ability. In fact, I was probably trying a bit *too* hard: I was so obsessive about being well presented and striving for perfection that I even ironed my socks and underpants!

Despite still being very homesick, I knuckled down every single day. The discipline and organisation in the Navy carried me through. I used it to my advantage, to help keep myself on track, while all the while reminding myself that I was here to stay. I was not going home and therefore I should work hard and make as big a success of this situation as I possibly could. What was the point in doing anything other than my best?

I had to dig very deep at times, especially when I faced physical challenges. In order to pass the fitness test I had to do a mile and a half run in under 11 minutes, swim 50 metres in overalls and hit tough targets in shuttle runs, burpees, sit-ups and a 300 metre shuttle run. On top of that there were academic exams and practical training tests to navigate. It was intense, but I gave it my all and passed every test. In fact, I'd done so well that I was awarded the Captain's prize. I still have the certificate, which states I achieved 'the highest standard of bearing, appearance and kit upkeep' in my class.

After six weeks I had completed my Part I training and had my passing out parade. I hadn't left the training camp in all that time and I'd become entrenched in Navy life. I felt part of a team, I was as thin as a rake and any thoughts of leaving had been banished from my head. I'd come this far, I wanted to stay and I was proud of my achievement so far.

My family and my girlfriend came to my passing out parade and didn't recognise me. I guess I wasn't a 'Kevin' anymore. I was focused and driven and I was full of pride when I marched to a military band, had my inspection and took the salute.

I bought myself a new kit bag and a Royal Navy tee shirt, which I loved wearing when I had time off at home. It was like a badge of honour and tethered me tighter to my new career. I couldn't leave now, not after I'd walked around in a Royal Navy tee shirt, telling my friends about all my adventures and my passing out parade! For some reason I also decided to take out a loan to buy myself a Mini, which was not one of my better decisions! I paid £1000 for it and signed a 'sold as seen' document. The only problem was, I bought it in the dark, and when I looked it the next day I realised it had been rolled!

After a short break I embarked on nine months of training at one of the primary shore airfields of the Fleet Air Training School (HMS Daedalus), which was in Lee-on-Solent, Hampshire. I'd already decided which branch of the Fleet Air Arm I wanted to work in: I'd seen *Top Gun* and I wanted to be in Weapons Electrical, otherwise known as WL, working on board harriers, tinkering with things like ejector seats.

I continued to work hard and now I also started to play hard, going out a lot with the other lads. I was earning about £1,000 a month and had no accommodation costs, so I could afford to go out on the beer on my nights off. I made good friends and was really enjoying myself, while continuing to put maximum effort into my training.

I worked extremely hard for all my exams and was praised for my efforts. I responded really well to the encouragement of the teachers and it motivated me. The only other time I'd had a boost like this was when Frieda, my English teacher, spotted I had some potential. It's so important to have a mentor, and I was just starting to figure this out. Rewards are important too. Back then I hadn't worked out that I could reward myself to help me reach my goals, but the Navy had it sussed; well, sort of!

After working my backside off for nine months I was presented with an award for 'sustained effort' and given a prize of a £10 road atlas. To this day, I have no idea what the thinking was behind giving a road atlas to a lad who about to sail around the world! I was very pleased nonetheless. I don't mind admitting I was not the brightest recruit and I was never going to win the maths prize. Just like at school, my attention span was definitely below average, and when it came to pure academic work I didn't excel.

What *did* work for me was the structure and discipline of Navy training. I responded extremely well to completing tasks that were set out in a clear and structured way, like bullet points in a book. I found I could concentrate hard and put in maximum effort when I knew precisely what was required of me and how long I had to perform a task: hence my success in bagging the prize for 'sustained effort'.

Once my training was complete I was assigned to HMS Invincible, based at RNAS (Royal Naval Air Squadron) Yeovilton in Somerset, home of the Red Arrows. From there I got to travel the world along with 1,100 other blokes, as it was in the days before women were permitted to work alongside men. Being on board HMS Invincible definitely increased my resilience.

For a month I worked eight days on, eight days off. The shift was from 8am to 8pm, and I could never sleep because our accommodation was right under the flight deck. There would be eight sorties a night, one after the other, taking off directly above my head. I was in a bottom bunk bed and there was such a small gap between my head and the bed above I had some horrible bouts of feeling claustrophobic, which didn't help either.

Waves of homesickness still washed over me from time to time, but I'd got used to it now. Though I missed my friends and family a lot I no longer pined to return home. Probably inevitably, my relationship with my girlfriend didn't stand the test of time, and we split up.

On a positive note I saved up a lot of money by being away at sea. When we docked and had a couple of days off it was beer time, and I had plenty of funds to pay for however much beer I wanted! I partied hard with my mates, usually drinking for two days solid. I made a lot of really good friends and got to travel to America, Spain, Italy, Norway and the Caribbean. I can remember drinking Pina Coladas on the beach in Barbados, thinking I was Del Boy! That was a highlight.

Another great Navy memory I have is of becoming the ship's barber. This happened by accident, after I'd perfected the art of using the clippers to give myself a classic Navy cut, with tapered sides and a flat top. One of my friends asked me to do his hair the same way, and before I knew it had a queue. In the end I charged £1 a time, so I had a good little sideline going on! I even got asked to do some of the stokers' hair one time. It was quite an honour to be invited into their company because lads like me were generally looked down on by the stokers, as we would only come on board when the ship sailed. As members of the Fleet Air Arm we were commonly known as WAFUS – an acronym for Weapons and Fuel Users. However, to the stokers those letters stood for 'Wet And F*****g Useless'.

'Fancy a can of lager?'

The stokers' mess was in the depths of the ship's hull. As soon as I arrived I was offered a small can of McEwan's Export.

'Great, cheers!'

I started work and four hours later, after more and more men had queued for a haircut, I'd made £20 and lost count of how many cans of lager I'd drunk. I left the stokers' mess after midnight, feeling decidedly half cut!

I enjoyed the camaraderie I continued to work hard and play even harder. The closeness I had with the friends I made in the Navy was priceless, although after a while I started to get fed up of the lifestyle, and in particular the binge-drinking that went hand-in-hand with every night off, when we went on shore. It was work, work, work on board the ship and alcohol, cigarettes and girls the rest of the time: there was nothing in-between. By the age of 20 I started to feel I wanted to break the cycle and move on to pastures new.

'Dad, I think the time has come for me to leave the Navy and get into the Fire Service.'

I can remember that conversation well. I'd matured and toughened up so much during my time in the Navy and I felt like I was talking to my dad man to man, and that he would approve and give me his blessing. I'd earned my stripes and proved myself in the Navy; that's how I felt.

By now my dad was a Senior Divisional Officer and had moved from Lancashire to take up this post with the Kent Fire and Rescue Service. He listened to me and agreed. I'd given the Navy four years and it had transformed me from a struggling, immature teenager into a fit and confident young man of the world. Dad had no concerns about me becoming a firefighter and thought it would be a good career move for me.

'Of course, son, but you'd have to apply to Kent, not Lancashire,'

I knew this. He and Mum had relocated together when Dad was promoted. I'd have no choice but to live with them as I had no home of my own, and the rule at the time was that you had to apply to the Fire Service in the county in which you lived. This was disappointing to me, as I'd have preferred to return to Lancashire and my dream would have been to work at the main Preston fire station, but it wasn't meant to be. I needed a roof over my head and my family around me, and so it was agreed I'd leave the Navy, move back in with my parents and apply to the Kent Fire and Rescue Service.

The next stage of my career was about to begin, although when I say 'next', at the time I thought it would be my *only* other big move. I envisaged that I'd rise through the ranks of the Fire Service like my dad and, ideally, stay there until I retired. I knew the pension scheme was second to none and you could retire earlier than in other jobs, with a very decent package. I'd grown up viewing the Fire Service as providing a job for life, and that was what I was ready to go into. After life in the Navy, I had no fears or doubts. I was excited and optimistic: this was what I'd always wanted to do, wasn't it?

LESSONS LEARNED FROM MY NAVY YEARS

Look after yourself. When I failed my Navy medical I got a sharp wake-up call. Take a look at your lifestyle and make improvements, because a healthy mind and body will help you produce your best work, and your best book. Although I still enjoy a beer every now and then, I often find I write my best books when I quit alcohol and junk food altogether. You'll be more productive and I guarantee you'll get more done!

Be a fighter, not a quitter. If I'd have got on the bus instead of walking home after failing my Navy medical I honestly believe I would not have achieved the success I have today. Face adversity with bravery and remember, many famous authors have overcome hurdles like poverty, rejection, illness and crippling self-doubt before successfully publishing their work. One of things I love about being an author is the fact you don't need any money to get started. All you need is a laptop and a desire to succeed. Another thing I have learned during my careers as an author and publisher is the need to maintain a positive attitude. I always try to surround myself with positive people and I have no time for negativity. By surrounding yourself with positive and supportive people you will have a much better chance of writing a bestselling book.

Use visualisation. When I thought of the humiliation I would feel if I had to tell my friends I was too fat to join the Navy it was a game-changer for me. I wanted to see myself proudly wearing my uniform, not licking my wounds, and I wanted others to see me that way too. Picture two versions of yourself: the struggling writer who never quite gets to finish their book and the successful, bestselling published author. Which one are you going to be?

Be disciplined and organised. Being disciplined and organised were massive parts of life in the Royal Navy and I didn't realise until later in life how much these skills would help me as an author. As an author, you need to have the discipline to write content regularly and you must be organised during the self-publishing process.

Don't be afraid of fear. When I joined the Navy I was terrified, but it was the best thing I ever did. Embrace the fear of putting pen to paper as you transform yourself into an author. It's an exhilarating journey, and the more you write the less fearful you will become.

Don't be afraid of what others think. Everyone has an opinion, and they are entitled to it! However, who and what you listen to is up to you. If someone doesn't think your book idea is a good one, ignore them. Trust in your instincts and set your sights firmly on your goal of becoming a published author.

BLOCK OUT ALL NEGATIVITY IN YOUR LIFE AND FOCUS ON YOUR WRITING.

Richard McMunn

CHAPTER 3 -
Becoming a Firefighter

My Navy training and experience had served me well. I flew through the selection process for the Kent Fire and Rescue Service and was assigned to White Watch in Maidstone after completion of the tough recruit training course. As it had been in the Navy, being issued with my kit was a highlight. I felt I'd arrived and gained an instant identity when I was wearing my firefighter's uniform.

With Dad as a senior officer I had to develop a thick skin, as right from the start people were talking behind my back, saying I'd only got in because of my dad's rank and position. I can remember thinking how unfair that was but I didn't let the comments bring me down. Instead I decided I had to work even harder to prove myself, so as to put paid to my detractors. It seemed the best way to tackle the situation, because who could carry on slinging mud when then saw how hard I worked, how dedicated I was to the job and how determined I was to be the best possible firefighter?

There were 21 lads on White Watch at Maidstone Fire Station. It had a reputation as a tough watch. The men had saved many lives and it was a very male, testosterone-fuelled environment. They were great characters too. A man called Mick Brooker was my officer-in-charge and he ran the watch with great efficiency. He was tall and in his mid-forties, and he had a great presence about him. Everyone respected Mick, and I looked up to him from the day I arrived.

Mick soon took me under his wing. He made me train hard, and he said he saw potential in me, just as Frieda the English teacher had, and some of my teachers at HMS Raleigh. I viewed Mick as a father figure and listened carefully to everything he said.

I was just six months into my two-year probation period when Mick called me over.

'Alright boysie,' he said, because that's how he addressed all the young firefighters. 'You are going to do a presentation on topography.'

'Am I?'

I wasn't concerned about the subject matter. I knew this was all about how fire fighters learn to quickly assess areas they are dealing with, such as the location of fire hydrants and how to get to a certain address in the event of a fire. I was well versed on the topic and felt confident I'd soaked up all the necessary information on topography in my training so far. But did I feel qualified to give a presentation on it? No Way! I still felt like the new boy. I'd never given a presentation like this in my life before and I told Mick I wasn't sure I was the right man for the job.

'Just do half an hour, that's all,' he said. 'You'll be fine.'

I was absolutely terrified of messing up and making a fool of myself and I hoped Mick would let me off the hook. On my first Christmas at White Watch I'd been subjected to one of the old-fashioned 'initiation' ceremonies that used to be common in the Fire Service, but are now a thing of the past. My challenge was to stand on a chair and have custard poured over me while I gave a speech. Needless to say it wasn't a pleasant experience and did absolutely nothing to encourage me to want to put myself forward as a speaker any time soon!

I'd also suffered the humiliation of falling for one of the oldest tricks in the book. I was told the bells that sounded at the fire station when we had a fire to attend had stopped working, due to a fault.

'The bells are broken, Rick. Here's the binoculars.'

'What am I supposed to do with those?'

'Keep watch, of course. Go up to the tower where you'll have the best vantage point and radio down if you see a fire anywhere across the town. It's what we always do when the bells aren't working.'

I peered through the binoculars for an hour, searching for signs of fire all over Maidstone, before I realised this was another classic initiation stunt. I had to laugh it off, because what else could I do? It was character-building, and it meant I was being brought in as part of the watch. I wanted to be in with the lads and so I quite rightly took it on the chin, just as I learned most of my colleagues had when it was their turn to be the butt of the joke.

Unfortunately, Mick was very serious about me giving a training presentation, and when I realised I wasn't going to get out of this I decided I had to make absolutely certain I would do a good job, so as not give my audience any grounds to take the mickey. I knew I needed to be as well prepared as possible to give this my best shot and so I put together some slides to present on the overhead projector. That way, I figured, the attention would not all be focused on me and I would have a set structure to work to.

I began to work on making a series of acetate slides. It was the first time I'd done something creative like this in a long while and I really enjoyed making the slides. In fact, I found myself spending far too many hours on them, making sure they were perfect and very professional-looking. I was really pleased with the finished results.

Looking back, art had always been loitering on the fringes of my life. At the age of seven I won a Christmas card competition, run by Debenhams. I was given a book token for my efforts and was as pleased as Punch. However, just like with my acting and love of music, in my youth it never occurred to me that I should pursue a creative job or indulge my passions. They were the fun things, but work was something that necessarily had to be serious, wasn't it? That's how I viewed the world for many years.

Anyhow, despite having the best possible slides and having rehearsed my presentation to perfection, I was still really nervous when it came to delivering it. I had no idea how my colleagues would respond to having a young and inexperienced firefighter like me giving them a talk, and I didn't have a clue if I'd get the tone or the style right.

To my relief, the presentation went down really well. I quickly got into my stride, and in fact I was reminded of being on the stage at school, when I performed in *Bugsy Malone* during my time at Chipping Campden School. I liked being in the spotlight and, just as I'd enjoyed organising the charity music concert at Balshaw's High School, I felt the same sense of satisfaction when my project came to together and I delivered it successfully.

'Do another one,' Mick said, almost immediately.

'What?'

I was pleased I'd done well, but I hadn't banked on this being an ongoing challenge for me. When I thought about it, however, I realised Mick was giving me a great opportunity. Like any good mentor, he'd spotted a nugget of talent and wanted to nurture it.

From that point on I delivered many more presentations, with Mick encouraging me every step of the way. He got me doing at least one a month, talking about firefighter operational procedures from every possible angle.

As soon as I'd completed my probation, Mick wanted me to take on even more day-to-day responsibility. He put me in charge of one of the fire engines during one particular shift, which was a step up, and he told me he thought I had potential to rise through the ranks if I wanted to, and that I should push myself.

I responded really well to Mick's encouragement. I admired and respected him and didn't want to disappoint him. His faith in me was giving me a lot of self-belief, and I was all ears when Mick advised me to start taking my firefighter exams in order to gain promotion as quickly as possible. He told me he thought I could be in charge of a Watch one day and, thanks to Mick, I felt confident in my ability and my reaction was, 'Yes! I can do it!'

I began to work really hard on my exams, and I mean really hard! I'd decided my aim was to become Station Officer, and I was incredibly driven to succeed. I put in all the hours I could and I also began to put myself out there in the community, volunteering to do charity work and help promote the image of the Fire Service. This too was something Mick instigated and encouraged me to do.

One day Mick received a request from an advertising agency that was putting together a publicity campaign for the Government's Citizen's Charter scheme. As the Kent Fire Brigade had been awarded a 'Chartermark' for giving good service to the public, the advertisers wanted a Maidstone firefighter to appear in their national TV and newspaper campaign.

'I'll do it!' I said straight away.

As I've said, I didn't mind being in the spotlight, and this sounded like a fun opportunity that would be good for my image. I was right, or should I say I was *almost* right. The campaign was a huge success, and I enjoyed being a part of it. All I had to do was be photographed up a tree, gently rescuing a rook with a broken wing. The image and an explanation of Kent's excellent public service record appeared in almost every national newspaper and ran on national television, urging other organisations to apply for the Chartermark. I also appeared in the local press, meeting the Citizen's Charter Minister Robert Hughes and posing with my rescue photo.

Hilariously, when one local newspaper reporter asked the question, 'Why was Mr McMunn selected?' someone in the Fire Brigade press office embarrassingly responded, 'He's cute. He's fit and handsome.' And that's why I said I was *almost* right about this being good for my image!

'Would you take part in a photo shoot for us?' I was then asked, by a journalist from Kent Today.

The journalist explained that, because of those comments from the press office, the paper wanted to run a fashion and lifestyle piece on me in their 'Looking Good' section.

'After modelling on TV and newspaper adverts, we thought you could prove your modelling worth by dressing up for Looking Good,' she went on.

I was taken aback.

'It'll be a bit of fun and you'll get some great photos out of it.'

'OK,' I agreed, trying to stick to the 'don't turn down an opportunity' spirit Mick had instilled in me, even though I knew full well the lads at the station would have a field day with this.

Doing the shoot was fun, to be fair. I modelled some designer jeans and a wool suit and silk tie and didn't think much more of it. However, when I saw the paper the following week I was so embarrassed. The headline was 'Firecraker Rick in action' and the article read, 'Cute, fit and handsome – not the usual tags applied by Kent's fire brigade when describing one of their men. But then they've never had a potential male supermodel on their books . . .'

How humiliating! I was so embarrassed. The lads did indeed have a field day back at the station, and I don't blame them. In fact, I never, ever lived it down! I wasn't really bothered, if I'm honest. It was a laugh and I didn't mind being the butt of the joke with the lads at the fire station. The experience certainly didn't make me shy away from other opportunities to get involved with events in the community. Mick spurred me on, always reiterating how beneficial it was to have a positive profile and go above and beyond your standard duties as a firefighter if you wanted to keep climbing up through the ranks.

Charity work was encouraged, and I organised a team of twelve trainee firefighters to clean cars for shoppers in Maidstone. After cleaning 800 cars and raising money for both the Fire Brigade Benevolent Trust and Hospice in the Weald, the lads and me appeared in the Kent Messenger under the headline 'Rick's dirty dozen'. I loved it; I had a sense of pride and standing in the community, both of which fuelled my ambition to rise to the top.

Next I organised a ladder-climbing event in a shopping centre in Chatham. This involved 24 Training Centre recruits and me scaling the equivalent height of Mount Everest on a fireman's ladder a total of 1,400 times, dressed in our uniforms. We raised nearly £2,000, and from there I started to dream up ideas for bigger challenges that would raise even more money for charity.

Memorably, I took a group of 22 recruits on the Three Peak Challenge. We scaled Scafell Pike, Ben Nevis and Snowden in three days, raising £6,000. We made the local paper again, which reported that the recruits were 'brimming with confidence and high morale' after completing the mission. This was what it was all about: everybody was a winner. The charities were happy, the lads and me had a great team-building experience, and all of our reputations within the Fire Service were boosted sky high.

I was also earning my stripes every single day at work. I put in 100% effort without fail. One day, when I was still in my early twenties, I was tested to the limit when I was called to what turned out to be the most frightening fire I ever attended. It happened when I was due to end my shift on White Watch one cold, Friday afternoon in winter. I was thinking about my plans for the weekend and looking forward to going out on the town with my mates when, all of a sudden, the bells went down and we were turned out to a fire in a furniture store called Clarke's in Maidstone town centre.

When we arrived black smoke was billowing out of the front entrance door and windows and a stressed shop owner was urging us to get a move on as his shop was in serious danger of burning to the ground. I hadn't dealt with such a potentially dangerous fire on a scale like this before, although my training had prepared me well. It was my turn to wear breathing apparatus, so I quickly got rigged up and followed the more senior firefighter I was with into the building. Straight away, I could sense something wasn't quite right. The smoke was becoming thicker and blacker by the second and the temperature was rising very quickly.

We had been told that the fire was probably in a room on one of the upper floors of the building so we quickly made our way up to the third floor, taking a hose with us so that we could tackle the fire. The hose would also help us retrace our steps on the way out. After about ten minutes the heat inside the building became unbearable and I couldn't see my hand in front of my face because of the thick, black acrid smoke. I concentrated on my training, took deep breaths and checked my air regularly. I was very fit at the time and hadn't used that much air from my cylinder. My colleague shouted in my ear that he couldn't see the fire anywhere and that maybe we should start thinking about evacuating the building due to the intensity of the heat.

Just as we started to retrace our steps we heard a noise that was every firefighter's worst nightmare: the sound of short blasts of an Acme Thunderer whistle. This meant the officer in charge, outside the building, had decided to initiate the evacuation procedure. Listening to the whistle, we knew we knew we were in trouble, and to this day the memory of it still makes the hairs stand up on the back of my neck.

My colleague and I quickly tried to retrace our steps, following the hose carefully. I'd started to become slightly disorientated due to the heat but I knew the hose reel would guide us back down the stairs, and to ultimate safety. How wrong could I be?

As we approached the top of the stairs the hose suddenly disappeared. My colleague turned to me and shouted that the hose had become trapped under some fallen furniture and he couldn't find the other end of it. We sat together and took deep breaths, contemplating what to do next, now that we had effectively lost our lifeline. The whistles were still blaring outside and we knew that the only way to get out of this burning building was to try as hard as possible to conserve our air and remain calm.

I had a girlfriend at the time, and all I could think about was how much I wanted to see her again. I was determined to push on and get out of the building to safety and I told myself that I was capable of doing so. My colleague and I decided to locate a wall, follow it and hope it would lead to the top of the stairs. To our relief we did find stairs, but there was a problem. We still couldn't locate the hose, which meant that this flight of stairs was not the flight we had used to gain access to the building in the first place. We both knew we had no choice at this stage: we just had to go down these stairs and hope they would lead us outside.

My heart was beating like never before. I feared the staircase could be leading us to a cellar or basement area, and that we would become fatally trapped. Thankfully, as we descended we began to hear voices, and they were getting louder. The officer in charge had sent in an emergency crew to help locate us. We met the other men halfway down the stairs and they then led us out to safety.

Once I was outside of the building I remember looking back at the store, which had already been half demolished by the inferno. Another few minutes in there and I would have been dead, that's for sure. As I took off my breathing apparatus set, which was caked in soot, the officer in charge looked over at me with a huge sigh of relief on his face. The relief I felt myself is indescribable!

I learned a tremendous amount from that incident. Firstly, I was shown how important it is to remain calm in every crisis situation. Even when things are really bad, the only way that you'll achieve a successful outcome is by staying calm and focused. Secondly, I learnt the importance of comradeship and teamwork. Break the rules, be unprofessional or disorganised, and things will go wrong, it's as simple as that!

Back at the station I continued to work hard and study for my promotion exams. Eventually, I secured a temporary promotion at the county's Training Centre. I was 23 years old and my title was Temporary Leading Firefighter – something I was very proud of. Mick was impressed at the standard of my presentations that he very quickly put me forward for a Leading Firefighter Instructor's position. Following an interview for the position, I got the job. I was starting to realise that, if I worked hard and persevered, I would get rewarded.

I loved every minute of the job at Training Centre, and I actually ended up spending four years in this and other similar posts, teaching people how to become professional firefighters and also running firefighter recruit training courses. I was also taking more exams so I could go for the next promotion and become a Sub Officer, which would mean being in charge of a Watch.

My career was going from strength to strength. Thanks to Mick's constant support and mentoring I now had it in my sights to eventually become a Station Officer in charge of a fire station.

Mick never stopped encouraging me every step of the way and I ran with every suggestion and opportunity that came along, as well as studying hard for every exam I needed to take in order to reach my goal.

My old school teachers would have been amazed if they'd seen how hard I worked. The lazy, undisciplined schoolboy I once was had gone through a dramatic metamorphosis. The Navy had instilled in me the value of discipline, being organised, determination and now the Fire Service was continuing to inspire and shape me. I always asked myself, did I want to achieve and succeed or didn't I? Did I want the kind of results I got in my GCSEs, or did I want to flourish in the Fire Service in the way I had done in the Navy?

It was a no-brainer. I wanted success more than ever, and I started to look at how I studied and how my brain worked, in order to get the best marks in my firefighter exams. I recognised that I could retain information much better if it was in a visual format, and especially if it was colourful. Mind maps were my answer, and I used them all the time to help me study and revise.

My hard work paid off every time. I became a Sub Officer but I didn't want to stop there, of course, and I continued to devote as much energy as I could to my job, and to my charity work. I'd enjoyed all the events I'd organised and was always happy to put myself forward to help promote the Fire Service. It was a win-win, as my charity work added value to my CV.

One of my proudest achievements was doing an Ironman, when I was 26. I called it the 'Rickathon' and swam two miles in Maidstone's Mote Park swimming pool before running a marathon and cycling for nine hours to Folkestone and back. It was very tough. I was into swimming and running but not cycling, and immediately after announcing I was going to take on the challenge I started to get cold feet about doing such a long bike ride. It was too late though – posters had already gone up in the station and money had started to come in. There was no going back and so I just had to dig deep and get on with it. I'm very glad I did. It was a fantastic personal challenge, and I raised £10,000 for Demelza House, a local children's hospice.

I was feeling great. Life was good, and at this point in time I imagined I'd spend my whole career in the Fire Service, just like my mentor Mick. After decades of devoted service, he had begun to talk a lot about all the big plans he had for his retirement, which he anticipated would start when he reached fifty. The pension scheme was excellent then, and the chance to retire early on decent money was a huge incentive to staff to stay put and see out their careers in the Fire Service.

Tragically, Mick's plans never came to fruition as he was diagnosed with cancer and died several years before he was due to retire. I was very shocked and upset. It was unbelievable that such a powerhouse of a man was losing his life too early like this.Before he passed away I went to visit Mick with the other members of White Watch and he told me and a few of the other lads, 'Live your life, boys. Take all the chances life gives you. Don't turn down opportunities.'

That was classic Mick, I thought. He'd been presenting me with opportunities and pushing me forward ever since I joined the Fire Service. But his words had a broader meaning now. He was telling us to take opportunities in the whole of our lives and not just at work. I took this to heart, and I never forgot what Mick said.

LESSONS LEARNED FROM BEING A FIREFIGHTER

Prove your critics wrong. When people were talking about me getting into the Fire Service because of my dad it made me work even harder to prove myself. Don't let anyone tell you that you can't write a book. You can and you will. Use any negative feedback to your advantage, and imagine silencing your critics by proving your worth and being a successful author. Visualise your book on sale on Amazon or on the shelf in Waterstones. In life, you will always come across negative people. Ignore them and always focus on you and your own path to success.

Learn from a mentor. I was very lucky that Mick Brooker took me under his wing and pushed me to make the best of myself in the Fire Service. If you don't have a mentor, find one fast! Every writer needs support and guidance and, as I have already stated within an earlier section of this book, you will achieve your goals much faster.

Take opportunities. I was very unsure of myself when I was first asked to give talks and presentations, but I'm so glad I pushed myself out of my comfort zone. The same goes for putting myself out there in the community, and in the press. As Mick showed me, life is too short and you should live life to the full. Always make the most of opportunities, whether it's giving a talk to a local group, promoting your book online or submitting a press release following the launch of your book. Like me, you will probably surprise yourself. At the very least, you will have story to tell!

Learn as much as you can. During the early years of my Fire Service career I took every opportunity to learn and develop my skills. As an author, I encourage you to do the same. If you get the chance to attend an author/ publisher training course, make sure you attend. If someone offers to teach you a unique way to promote your book, accept the invitation. By learning and developing your skills as an author, you will greatly increase your chances of achieving your goals and become a bestselling author.

Work hard. I worked extremely hard on my Fire Service exams and with my charity work because I wanted to rise up through the ranks as quickly as possible. Don't coast in your career as an author. Set goals, work diligently and be prepared to go the extra mile with everything: your writing, the selling and promoting your work and the raising of your author profile.

You work hard for someone else, so why not work hard for yourself? We all go to work to earn a living. Whilst we are there, we work hard for our employer by making them more money or by improving their business. Why not work just as hard for yourself, in your spare time? Start writing your book during your spare time and the rewards will follow.

Put your book on pre-order. One of the first things I teach aspiring authors during my book writing and publishing training courses is to get your book cover design created straight away before putting the book on pre-order. This is such a great motivator as it will give you a deadline for finishing your book's content in time for the launch.

Stay calm and be a team player. Tackling the dangerous blaze at the Clarke's furniture store showed me the true value of these skills. If things go wrong in the writing or publishing process, being calm and composed will help you focus on a solution. Getting on with the various people you have to deal with in order to get your book on the shelf or online is important too. Being kind, diligent and pleasant to work with (even if everything is done on email) will only add to your success.

WRITE GREAT CONTENT AND THE FINANCIAL REWARDS WILL FOLLOW.

Richard McMunn

CHAPTER 4 -
Joining a Band

I'd made good friends with another firefighter called Adrian Godley. We were on the same wavelength and when we weren't working we went out nightclubbing a lot together, having a good time. The shift pattern on White Watch was four days on, four days off, and we went out at least three times a week. Adrian lived in a big terraced house in Maidstone and eventually I moved in with him, renting a room. Adrian was always good to me and I enjoyed spending time with him.

One of the attractions of living with Adrian was that he said I could have a drum kit in the house. I hadn't played for years, not since I bashed about on my sister's boyfriend's sparkly drum kit back in Lancashire. I'd thought about drumming a lot over the years. Obviously, there was no chance of playing drums when I was in the Navy and was and sharing a bunkroom with a couple of dozen blokes! But now I had the opportunity to get myself a drum kit and get back into it, and I was going to make the most of it. I was very excited at the thought.

I bought a drum kit called Thunder. In hindsight it was absolute crap, but I loved it. I liked the fact it was black, my favourite colour, and it had a lightening stripe on the front bass drum skin. It didn't cost a lot of money because I didn't have much spare cash in those days. In fact, I was spending way more than I was earning and maxing out on credit cards. I think it was just my age, and the stage I was at in my life. In fact, I'd lost count the number of times I'd asked Adrian to lend me some money so I could go out nightclubbing! I was young, free and single and working hard and playing harder, just as I'd done in my Navy years. The difference was that I had more bills to pay than I did in the Navy, and I didn't really factor that in! Money had never motivated me and I didn't pay much attention to my financial affairs. What mattered was being able to do the things I loved.

From the day I got my Thunder kit I divided all of my spare time between practising drumming and going to the gym. I practised for hours and hours on end, and when I went to the gym I always gave it my all and pushed myself as hard as I could. I was determined to be the best drummer I could be, and I wanted to be as fit as possible too. My goals helped me stay motivated and disciplined and I was relentless in my pursuit of excellence.

I got the next promotion I wanted and started to run a Watch in Folkestone, as Sub Officer. This proved to be a steep learning curve for me. Some of the 20 or so men on the Watch were difficult characters to deal with. I think the fact I was still in my mid 20s perhaps didn't go down too well with some of the older guys. It didn't faze me, but I had to dig new depths of resilience to do my job well.

I stayed in Folkestone for approximately 12 months before transferring to another Sub Officer post in Gravesend. I liked the vibe there, and within a year I was promoted again, to Station Officer at Training Centre. This was an impressive achievement, as I'd risen very quickly up the career ladder. Part of my job was to help create application form and interview questions for people applying to join the Fire Service, which I enjoyed a lot because once again it allowed me to be creative.

My drumming soon started to take off too. After practising on my own and teaching myself as much as I possibly could I invested in a few lessons at Sharon Music in Gillingham, and after that I decided I wanted to join a band.

I started looking through adverts in the free ads newspaper that came through my door, to see if I could find a band that might be looking for a drummer like me. One advert caught my eye. The band was called Cold Tuesdays and I gave them a call.

'Sorry mate, you missed it,' I was told by the lead singer. 'We've already taken on a drummer. But why don't you come down to our next gig anyway?'

He explained that they were playing at a fairly rough pub in Tonbridge, which was about half an hour away from where I was living.

'OK, thanks, I'll come down.'

That was my gut reaction, even though I'd been told the band already had a drummer. I decided to follow my instincts, and I'm very glad I did. When I arrived I really clicked with all the lads and I liked the kind of music they did. It was all Beatles and classic hits and I was impressed. They let me do a few numbers and I loved it, and before I left the singer confided that they weren't sure about their new drummer.

A month later I took a call from the singer. He explained that the drummer they took on hadn't lasted, and he asked if I wanted to join Cold Tuesdays. 'Yes!' I said. I didn't need to think twice; I definitely wanted to join the band.

I loved doing gigs. We were typically paid about £100 between us for playing covers for a few hours in pubs and at weddings. There were normally six or seven guys in the band and of course we had to cover our own travel expenses and bar bill. This meant we just about broke even, or very often it was actually costing us all a few quid to be in the band! I didn't care. I wasn't in it for the money. The experience was fantastic, and I was improving my skills all the time. I'd always go to work on a high the day after a gig, and I felt that being in the band was a great antidote to some of the stress I dealt with at work.

The role of a firefighter was gradually changing. When I first joined the Fire Service the main focus was fighting fires and rescuing people from burning buildings. There were still days when how I performed as a firefighter could mean the difference between life and death, but now there were fewer fires. The job had a lot more to do with educating the public about fire safety and raising awareness about how to reduce the risk of fire in the first place. I was enjoying the job less as time went on, but it never occurred to me that I could leave the Fire Service and do something completely different.

I had been brought up watching my dad pursue his career in the Fire Service so doggedly that he moved the whole family around the country so he could take on promotions. Work and promotions were the way forward, weren't they? I did still believe this and I wanted to push myself and keep being promoted, although after Mick's death I think something had shifted. Looking back, I was more mindful of listening to my instincts and, ultimately, of making the most of all aspects of my life, and not just my career.

One night our keyboard player, Pete, couldn't make a gig and a guy called Simon Coulson stepped in. He'd been playing keys in another band and, like me, Simon was self-taught. He was also the same age as me and had a responsible job, having climbed up the corporate ladder in customer relations at BT, ever since joining as a school-leaver.

I liked Simon immediately. He was savvy and smart and seemed very calm and level headed. He joined the band full-time and we became really good friends. Simon didn't talk much about his job. He was commuting for two hour each way into London every day and working really long hours, and I got the feeling that when he was with the band the last thing he wanted to discuss was BT.

Unbeknown to me, Simon was in a rut at work. His job wasn't fulfilling him or inspiring him and he was ready for change, although he didn't fully recognise this just yet, or know exactly what that change was going to be.

Meanwhile I continued to do well in my job at Training Centre, and from there I was promoted again, to Station Commander at Ashford. On paper this was another impressive leap for me, but the job was very disappointing. I was more desk-bound than I'd ever been, there was more red tape to deal with and I found myself in a lot of stressful management situations. Getting decisions made was becoming increasingly frustrating and I felt there was a lot of negativity around some of the boring management meetings I was required to attend. The number of fire and rescue incidents had reduced further still, which of course was excellent in the big scheme of things, but this made my job even more humdrum and boring than I was used to. I was 30 now and had been in the Fire Service for nine years. Could I really see myself staying until retirement age? And if not, what else would I do?

In 2002 I went to see Coldplay perform at the Brighton Centre. Back then they were a new, up-and-coming band and they'd just released their second album, *A Rush Of Blood To The Head*. I went with Simon and we were both blown away by their performance and were buzzing as we drove back up the motorway to Kent in his BMW convertible.

If I could have read Simon's mind that night I would have known he was asking himself a question that was going to change the course of his life, and ultimately change mine too.

Wouldn't it be fantastic to start a tribute band to Coldplay? That's what Simon was thinking as we headed up the M23 and round the M25.

Tribute bands were really taking off back then, and a bit of research told Simon that though there were countless Abba and Beatles tribute acts, for example, there didn't appear to be a Coldplay tribute band in existence.

He phoned me the day after the Brighton concert and asked if I'd be interested in joining him in this project and creating a new Coldplay tribute band. I looked up to Simon and respected him. When he explained that we'd potentially get the chance to perform to bigger crowds, travel to much better venues and earn more than £100 between us I could see that, as usual, he was talking a lot of sense.

'I'm in,' I said.

He also asked a couple of other guys he'd played with over the years, and we got Dan Slowly to join us on bass, and Steve Jenner on guitar. Simon himself was going to be the lead singer as well as the keyboard player, and the name he came up with was Coolplay.

As Simon is the first to admit, we could very easily have laughed at his idea, taken the mickey or bottled it, but we didn't. We were open-minded guys and we all agreed that we had nothing to lose and should give it a go. Simon was delighted. He was hating his job at BT by now, and though I don't think any of us really realised it at the time – Simon included - he was looking for an exit and had no intention of seeing out his career there.

Simon, Dan, Steve and me spent quite a few months practising all the tracks from Coldplay's two albums. It wasn't easy learning the arrangements as they were more complex than most of the rock and pop covers we were used to performing, but we practised hard until we mastered them. All of us wanted to make this work, and by 2003 Coolplay was ready to face the world!

We played to friends for our first gig. It wasn't brilliant, but at least we'd taken the plunge. Coldplay were becoming more popular all the time and were now very big news, and it didn't take long for Coolplay to take bookings for some decent sized gigs. Within a few months, Coolplay were playing events like college graduation balls with audiences of 2,000 or more. For gigs like that the band charged £2,000, which of course was a giant leap in pay from what the pubs around Gravesend and Maidstone were giving us!

Surprisingly, one of our very early gigs was a university graduation ball at which we shared the bill with the Appleton sisters, who used to be in the band All Saints. This was a massive coup for us and word started to spread. Before long we were being asked to do more gigs than we could comfortably deliver, as all four band members had day jobs and other commitments outside of Coolplay.

Simon could make most gigs as they were usually at weekends and he generally only worked Monday to Friday, but he wanted to devote more of his time to the band. After nearly 14 years at BT he'd had enough, but how could he walk out on a well-paid career to play in a tribute band that, let's face it, might have a short shelf life?

He was thinking about this when an event happened that opened Simon's eyes and made him totally reassess his life. On his way home from work one evening Simon collapsed from exhaustion at King's Cross tube station. He fell down an escalator and blacked out, and when he came to his senses he realised this was a wake-up call, and that it was time to shake up his life and chase his dreams instead of being stuck in the rat race he had come to hate. Coolplay was riding high and we were earning as much from two gigs at the weekend as we did in our regular jobs. Simon made up his mind, there and then.

He took voluntary redundancy from BT and left in December 2003. His payoff would cover him for a year if he made some cutbacks and carried on doing Coolplay gigs, and in that time Simon planned to figure out some other way of earning money.

'What are you going to do?' I asked him. 'Got any ideas?'

At first Simon shrugged and said he didn't know. He then decided to invest 75% of his redundancy money in a Toyota Granvia MPV for the band, so we could all travel to gigs together instead of taking several cars crammed with kit. I admired the fact he had the confidence to do this in the circumstances, although I know some other people thought he'd simply lost the plot!

It wasn't long before Simon started to say he was running an online business from his spare room. He didn't give much away to begin with and I didn't want to press him in case he was sensitive about the fact he wasn't in full-time employment. However, Simon had a spring in his step he didn't have when he was at BT, and it soon became apparent he was doing rather well with his new enterprise.

'What is it then?' I asked. 'What are you selling? How does it work?'

I began asking loads of questions, typically when we were in the Toyota driving to gigs all around the country at weekends.

It turned out that Simon had invested the last few thousand pounds of his redundancy money in a property in Bulgaria, where houses were incredibly cheap at the time. He'd also been to a workshop in London about how to make money by selling information products and training guides. The seminar taught you how to get hold of DVD or CD sets with resale rights, and sell the sets at a profit by mail order.

Simon being Simon, he quickly realised he could create and sell his own information products, rather than buying the resale rights on a product somebody else had devised. He also figured it would be far more profitable to sell the information in the form of eBooks rather than as physical DVDs or CDs. Then came his real lightbulb moment: Simon decided to use the research he'd already done in order to buy his house in Bulgaria to create his first eBook. The book took him just a few weeks to put together and he called it the *Bulgaria Property Guide.* Then he taught himself how to build a simple website and began selling the eBook online. He did this using websites that appeared on Google results listings that directed people searching for such information to his website. The guide began selling like hot cakes, generating profits of £400 a day!

It was great to see Simon doing so well. Obviously the money was fantastic but, more importantly, I could see Simon was so much happier being self-employed than he had been at BT. His experience inspired me to reassess my own life.

My position as Station Commander in Ashford wasn't getting any more enjoyable; in fact I was finding it more frustrating than ever. The only part of my work I'd really got a buzz from was the training and recruitment side. However, as a Station Officer running my own fire station I no longer got to use my creative side and this was becoming more and more unsatisfying.

The reality was I'd have loved to become a full-time drummer, but I felt I simply couldn't afford to take that risk. I was earning £36k in the Fire Service by now and I had a company car, but I didn't have any savings. In fact, I had debts, because I'd wasted a load of money on stuff I had nothing to show for, like nights out, takeaways and holidays. Giving up a well-paid job was just not an option and, besides, I'd spent my whole life believing the smart thing was to have a job for life, which the Fire Service gave me.

Even though I was becoming increasingly fed up with my job in the Fire Service, I didn't let the situation get me down. I made an effort to be positive and focus my attention on what I loved - my drumming. I wanted to get better at playing the drums and in order to achieve this I needed to find a new drum teacher.

There was a young guy called Mat who was teaching drums in his spare time just up the road from where I lived in Maidstone. He played the drums to professional standard and I went along for a few lessons with him. I immediately got on well with Mat and we started chatting about work and what we did for a living when we both weren't playing the drums. As soon as Mat heard I was in the Fire Service, he responded with:

'I'd love to be a firefighter.'

'Really?' 'Yes, absolutely. I was wondering, can you teach me how to get in?'

I agreed, and we came to an arrangement. I'd coach Mat to ensure he would be as fully prepared as he possibly could be whilst going through the firefighter recruitment process, and in return he would give me some drum lessons.

It worked like a dream. I taught Mat all about the personal attributes and qualities he needed to demonstrate in his application and interview and took him through the whole recruitment process step by step. He got the job and was delighted – we both were. In fact, Mat is in the Fire Service to this day, and in his spare time he drums for Iggy Pop!

LESSONS LEARNED FROM BEING IN A BAND

Follow your heart. I instinctively knew I needed to take up drumming again, and I made it happen when I spotted the opportunity. Make sure you feed your creative needs and make every effort to continue with hobbies and pastimes, however busy you become. Being fulfilled and happy in your life will inform and improve your writing.

Follow your gut instincts. When I went to meet my first band, the Cold Tuesdays, I knew they had already found a drummer but I went anyway. Trust your instincts as a writer and author. They don't usually let you down.

Think outside the box. For many years, I thought I'd be a firefighter for life and I didn't challenge this. I was surprised that I could be a writer in addition to doing my job in the Fire Service, and stunned when I found a new career I loved more than anything I'd done before, and that would change my life. If you really want to write and publish a book, what are you waiting for? Whatever your age, don't wait for someone else to give you permission. Make it happen, even if that means changing your lifestyle or previous life goals.

Be open to ideas and think big. When we formed Cooplay we put in hours and hours of work with no guarantee of success, but I liked the idea, was prepared to work hard and I had a positive attitude. Be an open-minded writer. Be a brave author. And think of what CAN happen, not what might go wrong.

YOUR BOOK COVER DESIGN IS CRITICAL TO YOUR BOOK'S SUCCESS.

Richard McMunn

CHAPTER 5 -
Creating How2Become

'What are you going to do next?' I asked Simon.

We were on our way to a gig and, as usual, I was picking his brains. It was fascinating to hear how Simon was running his new Internet business, and I wanted to hear the next instalment in his story.

'Oh, I'm doing some information products about how to qualify as a plumber,' he replied casually.

I knew that Simon had created several other property guides since his original *Bulgaria Property Guide,* and he explained that he'd started to widen his net after running out of countries to cover, turning his hand to producing eBooks on a range of other subjects.

'How to qualify as a plumber? What gave you that idea?'

Simon explained that he'd read a newspaper article about how a City trader gave up his job and re-trained as a plumber, because plumbers were in high demand and earning great money. The story had stoked a great deal of interest in plumbing courses, and Simon saw a gap in the market. He quickly created an eBook on the subject and it sold like hot cakes. In fact, Simon's guide was so popular that he also brought out an accompanying DVD and eventually went on to run a training course on how to become a plumber.

The day after Simon told me about his plumbing products I went on the website he'd created to sell them from, and that's when a light went on in my own head.

'This is genius!' I thought, looking at the website.

I'd already spent months listening to Simon and thinking, 'What could I do if I went down his path?'

Now it was blindingly obvious. I should create an information product on how to become a firefighter. I already had all the content at my fingertips. I was a specialist in this subject and had been training recruits and writing interview questions and tests for would-be firefighters for many years. What's more, I'd also had recent success with my drum teacher Mat, who had effectively had one-to-one coaching from me on how to enter the Fire Service. Mat wasn't the only person I'd mentored over the years. Countless people had asked me for my advice, so much so that I had ended up burning a lot of information onto a CD so it was easier to share with all the friends and friends-of-friends who asked for my help. I had done that purely to make it easier to share the information, never realising the real value of what I was handing out, or that I was actually mentoring people.

The next time I saw Simon I asked him loads more questions, and he suggested I went to his house one afternoon so he could show me the ropes about how to create an eBook to sell online. After asking me what I wanted to write about he agreed wholeheartedly that a 'how to become a firefighter' book was the obvious choice: the best ideas are often right under your nose, we conceded.

In just a few hours Simon taught me how to set up a simple website with a PayPal button on it, and how to drive traffic to the site using Google advertising.

On Boxing Day 2004 another light went on when I realised I could write many more 'how to become' titles. In fact, I could create a whole business called 'how to become'! I was watching the shocking footage of the tsunami on the news when the thought first struck me. I have no idea what triggered it – perhaps it had something to do with seeing the various emergency services in action on the TV. Whatever my thought process was, I realised I didn't just have to write about how to become a firefighter. I was also qualified to write about how to get into the Royal Navy, and why stop there? If Simon could write about plumbing when he wasn't a plumber, I could research other jobs and careers too, and fill many other gaps in the market to help people get the jobs they wanted!

My mind was racing and I had goosebumps on the back of my neck as I thought this through. I was emotional, listening to the news and seeing the pictures coming in from Thailand, and I was also feeling extremely motivated and excited. I was going to help people change their lives! It was really invigorating.

I immediately started playing around with the words 'how to become' and quickly settled on naming my new business 'How2Become'. It was so simple and so perfect! I was buzzing, and incredibly optimistic about how this business was going to turn out.

I naturally wanted to call my website 'How2Become' and I immediately checked to see if the domain name was available. I wanted 'how2become. com' but this was unfortunately already registered to an American. It meant I had to settle for how2become.co.uk in the short term, with a view to buying the name from the American in the future – which I'm happy to say I eventually did.

Next I started to think about how my website and branding would look, and I realised I needed a logo. From the coaching I'd given Mat and others over the years I understood it was essential to have two key elements in the type of information book I was going to sell, because it was a tool someone would use to take a big step in their life. I knew the content must be excellent and, just as importantly, I realised the content had to lead the reader to a point of personal transformation, whether from City trader to plumber or from office worker to firefighter. I thought about this and decided to have a logo showing three diamonds slanting to the right. The idea was that the slanting diamonds would reflect the quality of the content and the progression you could achieve from reading my books. I had never been involved in logo design before but I didn't let that put me off. Armed with my idea I bought a piece of software, followed the instructions and was pleased with the slanting diamonds logo it helped me create. I was all set to get my website built and launched, but first, of course, I needed my first product to sell!

It was time to sit down and write the content for *How to Become a Firefighter* in a style that would suit an eBook and be most useful and user friendly for the people it was written for. There was a cellar in my house, and I decided that would be a good place to work. It meant that whenever I had free time I'd be able to shut myself away and focus on the writing without any distractions. I drove to a local MFI store, bought myself a chipboard desk and installed it in the cellar, which became a great bolthole from where I could write my first book.

I installed myself at the desk and opened a new Word document on my old Hewlett Packard computer. The scene was set; even my black cat Sooty was at my feet, looking at me in anticipation. That's when a scary thought hit me. *I'm not a writer. What am I doing?*

The situation suddenly seemed a bit absurd as well as daunting. How was I going to write a book? I was an ex-Navy lad turned firefighter. I'd scraped a C grade in my English GCSE and I had no experience of being a writer, author or indeed publisher.

I took a deep breath and typed the title of my book: *How to Become a Firefighter.* I'd made a start, at least. Next I told myself not to panic! I reasoned I had already started on this journey and I had to see it through, no matter how unsure I was about my ability to actually write a book.

When I slowly began filling the pages I found the process exciting and I began looking forward to getting into the cellar and sitting at my desk at every opportunity. What helped massively was that I worked out an action plan in the beginning which made me see the book as a collection of sections, rather than one huge document, which would have been alarming.

I knew that as well as describing the practical steps and the nuts and bolts of the Fire Service application process I needed to give the book a unique selling point – a USP. Clearly, the fact I was a serving firefighter was my USP, and I recognised I needed to capitalise on that. To do this I branded the book with the words 'The Insider'. I was already thinking I could potentially create an 'Insider' series of books if this one worked out. I just hadn't yet worked out exactly how I would do this, given I only had inside knowledge of the Fire Service and the Navy! I was also careful to make sure the book truly offered the reader the inside knowledge that could transform their life. This needed to be a product for people who were serious about applying for a job in the Fire Service, and who wanted to give themselves the best possible chance of success.

The content for *How to Become a Firefighter* came to me very easily, because I knew it all off by heart. I was very used to talking about how to get into the Fire Service and I had years of experience of writing bullet points on slides, making lists of interview questions and training new recruits. Effectively, all I really had to do was decide on my word count and the various headings and sections I wanted to include and write them up to the correct length. This way I could give myself reasonable targets and achieve goals every time I sat down to write. It meant I would end a writing session feeling satisfied I'd written 100% of what I'd set out to do, instead of feeling I was still only 5 or 10% through the entire book.

It took me about three months to finish *How to Become a Firefighter*. It was 300 pages long and I was incredibly proud of my achievement. I immediately started selling it on my website, in the form of an eBook on a CD. I did this by burning the content onto a CD, printing off a sticky How2Become logo and adding an insert to the CD case with a bit of information about the product and How2Become. The CDs looked great, and I was really pleased with the product as a whole. I felt it was very good value for money because I was confident it would do exactly as it promised: it would help you become a firefighter if that is what you wanted to be.

LESSONS LEARNED FROM CREATING HOW2BECOME

Recognise your mentors. When I met Simon I didn't instantly regard him as a mentor, but he was. As a businessman he was inspiring, and I soon recognised that I could learn from him. Never pass up the chance to learn from a mentor. Be keen, stay interested and keep asking questions. Again, if you don't have a mentor, find one.

Don't be put off by obstacles. When I realised How2Become.com was not available as a domain name I wasn't deterred and thought positively about how I could get around this. The same went for designing my logo and teaching myself how to burn CDs and package them. You need a *can-do attitude* when writing and publishing. Trust in the phrase 'where there's a will there's a way': it will help you achieve your aims.

Get into the zone. Buying a cheap desk and working in my cellar was a great move for me as I felt poised and ready to write whenever I sat there. Make yourself comfortable and find a space and time that works for you. There are so many different places you can write as an author, including your local coffee shop, library, home office or bedroom and even your car during your work lunch break! All you need is a laptop to get started. You should also think carefully about the time of day you are most creative. Some authors prefer to write very early in the morning, whereas others (me included) prefer to write late at night.

Be brave and focus on your strengths, not your weaknesses. I believed in my USP as I knew people would benefit from my guides and that they could transform a person's life. Even though I was not the most confident writer I knew I could write content for presentations and CDs, as I'd already done it. Believe in your work, focus on giving the reader great value for money and think about what you have written successfully before.

You have nothing to lose, so start writing now! Don't be one of those people who constantly finds excuses for not achieving their goals. There is always time to write during the day. Even if you just manage to write one page a day, it is still PROGRESS.

SWAP WATCHING TV AND SURFING THE INTERNET FOR WRITING CONTENT.

Richard McMunn

CHAPTER 6 -
Becoming a Businessman

When I made my first sale of *How to Become a Firefighter* I was absolutely buzzing! I'd spent about £50 on Google Ads and I was selling the CDs for £12.99 each so I wasn't yet in profit, but I was confident my product was going to do well. At the time, back in 2005, I was paying 7p per click to Google, meaning that every time a customer made a purchase after being directed from a Google Ad, that's how much I had to pay them back. I didn't really have much of a clue about this type of stuff and was on a steep learning curve, to tell the truth. Simon was still helping me a lot, and I kept looking at his plumber website and some others he had running, to see how he was promoting his products and pulling in customers.

One thing Simon mentioned very early on was that I should start to build up a mailing list, as this could be used for future marketing. I followed this advice, and in time it came in very useful.

Sales continued but it was a slow burn in the beginning. I still had a lot to learn about how to drum up business. I started placing ads in newspapers, although in hindsight this was not my best idea as most people reading newspapers are not looking to buy a product like mine. A person serious about finding such specific information is much more likely to go online and Google some keywords, so I began to educate myself more about how to get my business at the top of the relevant Google searches.

I also learned about the value of giving away free bonus products in order to boost sales. For example, in time I wrote a fitness guide – *How to Get Firefighter Fit* – and I gave it away as a freebie. Later on I included it as a bonus chapter in updated versions of the main firefighter book. I was learning all the time! Looking back, these were such invaluable lessons to learn so early on in my writing career: updating books regularly and giving extra value in new editions are crucially important to success.

It wasn't long before I was selling 30 copies of *How to Become a Firefighter* every day of the week, which was SO exciting. I'd clearly found a gap in the market and I had high hopes for the future. If this book worked, I was sure other titles I'd already thought about would sell too. Having this outlet for my creativity and seeing my first book sell was extremely inspiring, and I couldn't wait to get started on my next one.

As well as thinking ahead I needed to look after my existing customers. The CDs all needed to be packaged and posted out to customers and with sales averaging over 200 CDs a week this had become quite a task. I can remember driving round to post the orders in lots of different post boxes as I was filling them all up! It was clear I needed help. Pete, a good friend and former colleague of mine from the Fire Service, offered to pack the Jiffy bags and help me with the accounts, and in return I gave him some shares in my newly formed company. It was great to have him on board and it allowed me to focus on my writing rather than on packing Jiffy bags and dealing with customer queries and accounts.

Even though I was making a lot of money from the sale of the CDs, and I had high hopes of replicating my success with future publications, at this stage I didn't consider leaving my job in the Fire Service. It felt way too early to be thinking along those lines, even though the prospect of being my own boss and spending all the time I wanted on growing How2Become was very appealing. The result was that I'd often find myself staying up researching and writing until 3am, all after doing a full day at work. I didn't mind; in fact I was thriving because I was doing something I thoroughly enjoyed. It usually felt more like a hobby than work, despite the fact I was already earning more from my book sales than I was in the Fire Service. I was being creative once more, and as such I felt truly fulfilled.

With the exception of one or two close friends I told nobody at work about How2Become. To create *How to Become a Firefighter* I hadn't used any specific material that belonged to the Fire Service and I wasn't doing anything illegal, but for the time being I wanted to keep my business secret. This seemed appropriate given the book was written by an 'Insider' and in any case, from now on I was going to be writing about other jobs and careers completely outside of the Fire Service, so why did my colleagues or bosses need to know about my business?

For my second book it made perfect sense to stick to my tried and tested formula, and as I've already mentioned my obvious second title would be about how to join the Royal Navy. I found that I wrote this book much quicker than the first, as I was effectively replicating the process but with different content. The fact I'd passed the Navy selection process myself was priceless and I still had some sample Navy tests I'd used when I was younger. This time I also had to do some research to make sure everything I included in the book was up to date, but I wasn't daunted. Having a clear plan and structure laid out and knowing what information I needed to find, and how to present it, made the process relatively simple.

When *How to Join the Royal Navy* started selling well on CD too I felt I was on a roll, and my mind was working overtime. Clearly, I needed to come up with another book idea, but what could I do next? The only other job I'd done, besides being in the Navy and the Fire Service, was to run my own mobile car wash business as a teenager! I couldn't write 300 pages on how to fill buckets of water and knock on neighbours' doors, so what was the answer?

I thought very logically about this. My books had to give 'Insider' information – that was my USP. I wanted people to get value for money and actually get the job they wanted after reading my guides. That was crucial to my brand and was something I felt very passionately about. Therefore, I had to get hold of the insider knowledge my books needed, and the only way to do that was to apply for jobs and experience the recruitment process in different careers first hand.

I sat down at my MFI desk once more, and this time I began filling out job application forms. Labour was in power and the public sector was recruiting all the time. Some quick and simple research showed me that jobs in the probation service were popular and so I applied for a job as a probation officer. I went through the whole process, including an assessment and interview, and afterwards I was offered a £14k a year job, which of course I turned down. Crucially, I took loads of notes throughout the process and kept a diary about what I'd learned, how I felt and what the key tips and pointers were for other candidates. After my interview I ran to the car and wrote down every single question I'd been asked, plus any other detail I could remember that I thought might be useful to prospective candidates.

Later, I replicated this process with applications to join the Police and to become a Police Community Support Officer (PCSO). I also went on to cover other popular jobs like train driver, train conductor and cabin crew, and I applied to become a Highways Agency Traffic Officer, a prison officer and a paramedic. For the latter I also tapped into the experience of a friend who worked for the Ambulance Service and was happy to help.

Around this time the Fire Service gave me the opportunity to do a Diploma in Management Studies. I didn't really want to do it as I knew it was quite a tedious course, but I felt I ought to. I then realised I could turn it to my advantage, by writing my dissertation on how Fire Service recruitment policy compared to that of the Armed Forces! In researching my chosen subject I was able to secure some key meetings with recruitment staff from the Armed Forces, and I got to see their scoring criteria. Later on this helped me no end when I went on to write various Armed Forces guides, and the diploma itself helped me improve how I structured content.

As I'm sure you can imagine, I was a very busy man. I was devoting every spare minute to applying for various jobs and going through the stages of the different selection processes, tests and interviews. It was very stressful and at times I felt a bit like an undercover reporter who might get rumbled at any moment! I managed to keep my nerve when the going got tough by telling myself I was doing this for a useful purpose and that I needed to get hold of the best possible information I could, to justify putting 'Insider' on my books and to give my customers what they wanted.

More often than not I was offered the job I applied for. If I wasn't successful I always asked for feedback on how I could improve and what I needed to do to get the job next time round. This happened when I applied to the RSPCA and failed at the testing stage, after finding the verbal comprehension test very difficult. The feedback I got on my performance became an invaluable source of information for my next book. I always made sure I used this golden opportunity to ask for feedback. This kind of knowledge, from the horse's mouth, was exactly what I had set out to find: advice and guidance from the inside. This was my USP, and this is what I wanted to give to my readers, to provide them with a product that was great value and could potentially transform their life.

I had the occasional legal letter to contend with. The RSPCA, for example, did not like me using their name and so I had to make some modifications to my text and talk about 'animal inspector' or 'pet inspector' instead, and the Probation Service also got wind of what I was up to and wrote to me to tell me as much. Their letter really worried me until I carefully studied the wording. It was actually nothing more than a formal letter of complaint rather than a serious threat of legal action, so I had nothing to really worry about.

I became more and more efficient at writing my books and I was also looking at how I could improve my website. People buying my first book knew I was a firefighter first and foremost, not a publisher, and therefore did not expect me to have an amazing website. I felt it was a bit too rough and ready though, and as I wrote more titles I wanted the website to be a lot more polished and clean-looking.

In the early days I was also proofreading all my own work, which is never ideal. Inevitably I missed a few spelling mistakes and so on, but I found that people were very forgiving, no doubt because I emphasised the fact I was still working for the Fire Service. In some ways this went in my favour: it was clear the guides were written from an authentic insider and not generated by a professionally trained copywriter.

For the first couple of years of running How2Become I produced about 30 eBooks in the same vein, still doing almost everything myself, apart from the packing and accounting, which my mate Pete still helped me with.

By 2006 I had 20 guides on sale via my website and the other 10 I'd written were going through the process of being put on to CDs. At this point I saw an advert online that caught my eye. It appeared as a banner on Yahoo, and it was advertising something called the HSBC Start-Up Stars award. I was a start-up and I wanted to be a star, or at least a winner! I clicked on the link to find out more.

LESSONS LEARNED FROM RUNNING MY BUSINESS

Persevere. I had no idea about advertising my books but I did my best online and in the local press. Sales didn't take off overnight, but I kept plugging away. Be determined, believe in yourself and your product and keep persevering until you get results. If you want to be a successful author, you *can* be.

Delegate. I didn't try to do everything myself and got help with my accounts and distribution. Don't be afraid to ask for help, but DO take your time, choose who you work with very carefully and always make sure you work with people you trust and get on with. In a later section of my book, I will teach you some valuable lessons about using outsourcers during the publishing process; make sure you read it as it will help you on your journey.

Watch what you say. When you have a successful business or a great book idea, people can become green-eyed. I've learned to choose carefully what to tell people. Keep your ideas for your books close to your chest until the book is either published or on pre-order.

Build on your success. Once I'd written one book it was so much easier for me to repeat the process with my second book. Look at what you have already produced and think how it can help make your job easier next time round. I am always encouraging first-time authors to think about their next book from the get go. If you have an idea for a 'series' of books, go for it!

Never take your eye off your reader. Once I'd exhausted writing about the careers I had first hand knowledge of I didn't use second hand information, I went out and found more first hand knowledge! Always focus on quality and giving your reader excellent value for money, and NEVER claim to offer anything that isn't actually in your book.

Be an opportunist. Right from the start I was always looking out for ways to expand and improve my business, whether through boosting my personal knowledge or revamping my website and looking for ways to raise my profile. No matter what stage you are at in your journey to becoming an author or publisher, never be complacent. Keep striving to improve, and your determination and hard work will shine through in your books.

WRITE CONTENT THAT TRANSFORMS THE LIFE OF YOUR READER.

Richard McMunn

CHAPTER 7 -
Becoming an Award-Winner

The HSBC award I saw advertised online was offering a top prize of £25k and the title 'Start-Up Star 2006'. It was nationwide and open to all businesses less than three years old. Competition was going to be stiff, but what did I have to lose? I didn't expect How2Become to win and the money wasn't what motivated me. I figured the exposure my business would get and the networking opportunities I might have access to were worth competing for.

When I started the application process I was taken aback. I was being asked to answer questions on my business plan and my precise goals in the short term, medium term and long term. This was all uncharted territory to me! All I did was write guides and sell them through my website, and I didn't have all these business plans written up. Nevertheless I persevered with the application, giving the best answers I could.

Happily, there was a question about How2Become's USP. Now I was on more familiar ground, and I explained with confidence how I gave my customers inside knowledge from my personal experiences in the Fire Service and Royal Navy, and how I put myself through selection processes for jobs I had no first-hand knowledge of. I cited the Probation Service as one such fact-finding application (and in fact that's how I got the legal letter I mentioned in the last chapter!)

For the next stage of the application I was asked to give a presentation at Canary Wharf, which felt a bit like being on *Dragon's Den.* Some of the questions I was asked really made me think about where I was going with my business.

'Why are you still a firefighter?'

'How can you concentrate on your business while you also have a full-time job?'

These were valid questions. The truth was, I was having my cake and eating it, and the panel could see that and said as much. I took their point but, privately, I didn't really see the benefit in rushing to give up my job with the Fire Service. I was managing perfectly well to juggle my role as a firefighter with being a writer and producer of information CDs, so why not continue in the same was for as long as I possibly could? At the very least I figured the excellent Fire Service pension was worth holding on for.

'You won't need a pension!' Simon always laughed. 'You're going to make millions!'

I hoped he was right, but I wasn't cut from the same mould as Simon. He'd walked away from his corporate job at BT even *before* he started his new Internet business, but I was not such a big risk taker. As a firefighter I was well used to taking *calculated* risks, and I didn't see the need to lose my safety blanket just yet.

After the Canary Wharf presentation it was clear that How2Become wasn't going to be the overall winner of the Start-Up Stars Awards, but I hadn't ever expected to win and had no regrets whatsoever about entering. I told myself I'd done well to get this far and then, to my absolute surprise and delight, How2Become was named as one of six South East regional winners who were put forward to the National Judging Panel. This was great news! What's more, after previously paying for newspaper adverts to promote my products I was now being asked to give interviews and pose for photos for the press.

Kent News ran a half page article and then the Kent Messenger wanted to do feature too. I agreed, thinking only about all the benefits the publicity would bring for How2Become. However, when I came to do the interview I realised there was no way I could do this without talking about the fact I was still working as a firefighter. The reporter who would interview me for the article was very interested in the fact I used my inside knowledge to start How2Become. I'd been very open and honest about this to everyone involved in the Start-Up Awards, but I'd continued to keep quiet about my business at work. Very few people knew what I did when I wasn't being a firefighter, and I wanted to keep it that way. I wasn't sure how my business would go down with my colleagues or bosses and still did not see the point in sharing what I did in my own free time.

I decided to do the interview anyway and, rather optimistically, I crossed my fingers and hoped that the resulting article would not be spotted by anyone at work! The Kent Messenger ran their story in August 2006, a few months before the grand final of the competition. The article filled half a page and included a colour picture of me and Pete plus a headline stating our job guides were 'red hot sellers'. There was also a reference to how I'd been 'burning the midnight oil' writing my career books when I wasn't doing my day job as a firefighter.

When my mum phoned me up to tell me she'd seen me in the paper I immediately knew the article wasn't going to slip by unnoticed at work. I wasn't wrong. I was called into a meeting with the unimpressed Assistant Chief, who was holding the article in his hand when I walked in the room.

'You need to decide. Do you want to be a firefighter or an entrepreneur?'

I'm a stubborn person and I stood up for myself, pointing out that lots of people had second jobs. Many firefighters worked as fire safety risk assessors, for instance, but this didn't cut any ice. I was told in no uncertain terms that my business was different: it was prominent and there was a conflict of interest. I wasn't being sacked, but I was being told what to do.

I left the meeting knowing that I was going to carry on with How2Become regardless. I also realised that even though I wasn't going to be dismissed, I would never get promoted within the Fire Service again. I wasn't worried about this. I had already achieved my big ambition, by becoming one of the youngest serving Station Officers in Kent at the time I got promoted, at the age of 29. I was 35 now and I was definitely less enthusiastic about being a firefighter than I had been all through my 20s. Nevertheless, I wasn't ready to quit the career I'd worked so hard for. It was still early days for How2Become and my head was full of ideas for future books and ways to expand the business. I wanted to carry on juggling both parts of my life, and that was what I was going to do.

An invitation dropped through my door shortly after that meeting with the Assistant Chief, inviting me to a champagne reception and dinner at the Savoy, where the winner of the Start-Up Stars Awards would be announced. Was I going to toe the line with my bosses at work and politely decline the invitation? Absolutely not! I was really looking forward to the event, and I was excited about the opportunities it might open up to me.

How2Become was only 18 months old at this point and I felt a real sense of achievement when I turned up at the Savoy as a regional winner. The Start-Up Stars Awards were backed by the Daily Express and Sky News and there was a great sense of ceremony and expectation in the air. I loved being part of it.

As I anticipated, How2Become didn't win on the night but I was simply glad to be there, and I was determined to make the most of this golden opportunity to network. One of the judges was Sally Preston, the hugely successful entrepreneur behind the frozen baby food company Babylicious. I went up to her at the end of the ceremony and asked if I could arrange a meeting with her, to find out how I could improve my business.

She agreed to give me a few hours of her time, and it was incredibly valuable to me. Sally said she felt my website needed to change as it looked quite amateurish, which I knew was true. If I'm honest, it looked like Del Boy had lashed it up! This had been fine when I was just selling my *How to Become a Firefighter* title and wanted people to recognise there was a real firefighter behind the guide, but now I had 30 different titles I needed a more professional image. Sally also pointed out that the fact I only worked part-time on the business also needed to change. Clearly, quitting the Fire Service and committing myself completely to How2Become would drive the business forward much faster, and productivity and profits would rise.

I hung on Sally's every word and decided there and then that I wanted to invest in a new website and really throw myself into building on the success of How2Become. I still wasn't quite ready to give up my full-time job, but I didn't think this was as big a barrier to future success as Sally and other business people I'd met through the Start-Up Awards thought it was. Like I say, I'm stubborn, and this was one decision I was sticking to, at least for the time being.

I told Pete I wanted to find an agency to build a fantastic website. We were turning over £1,000 a day on a good day and I thought spending some of our considerable profits on a top quality website, as well as improved branding, would be well worth the investment in the long run. Pete wanted to carry on as we were as we were already making good money, and I could totally understand his viewpoint. However, the entrepreneur and writer in me simply could not accept this. I wanted to write more and more books and I certainly didn't want to stand still. I wanted to grow the business, and I loved the excitement of it all. It wasn't about money, because I was already making great profits. This was about me being a driven and determined person, just as I'd been ever since my Navy training. I was prepared to work hard to be the very best in my field, and I did not want to settle for what I considered to be second best.

'I want to win more awards,' I told Pete. 'I want to have an amazing website. I want to write more books. I want to help more people apply for the job they want, and to turn their life around!'

I was extremely passionate about How2Become and, particularly after the dressing down I'd had at work, I was starting to really envisage a future in which I was a full-time writer and publisher. It was where my heart lay, and I was not prepared to take my foot off the accelerator at this crucial point on my journey. I had so many hopes and ideas. For instance, I had already started to think about expanding into areas like career mentoring and writing eBooks for foreign markets. In short, I saw a world of exciting possibilities, but it had become clear Pete saw things very differently, which I can understand. He was older than me and had retired from the Fire Service. Everybody is different, and at this point Pete chose to leave the business. I bought out the shares he had in How2Become, and now I was a lone wolf!

By now Simon was in the process of setting up his Internet Business School (IBS), through which he provides training and mentoring for people running online businesses. Mentoring me had been one of the catalysts for the creation of the IBS because through coaching me, Simon realised he had valuable skills and the ability to share his knowledge with others, including complete Internet novices.

Anyhow, I was lucky enough to be his friend, and Simon provided me with some excellent guidance and advice for free – or sometimes for the price of a few beers when we were out on a Coolplay gig!

'You're not setting up auto-responders,' Simon told me. 'Where's your mailing list and what are you doing with it? You should be upselling!'

He explained that auto-responders are those 'thank you for your order!' kind of emails that are triggered by a sale. Then he looked at my mailing list, which had grown to contain hundreds and hundreds of email addresses of former customers and people who'd been on my website.

'You've got a very decent-sized mailing list, so you should do a course,' Simon told me.

By this he meant that I should set myself up as a mentor, and his idea completely made sense. It was what I'd been doing at work for many years. I had vast experience of giving talks and presentations about firefighting, and now I had in-depth knowledge about a range of other jobs too. The people on my mailing list were my target audience, and it made perfect sense that I should offer them courses. Simon knew me well. We regularly shared a stage together with Coolplay, and he knew I was not fazed by the prospect of standing up in front of a room full of people and giving talks about how to navigate various recruitment processes.

Seeing how Simon's business was flourishing provided me with a lot of inspiration. His Internet Business School was doing extremely well. He was flying high, and I wanted to imitate his success. Thankfully, Simon had faith in my business and what it could achieve. He bought some shares in How2Become, and his investment and backing was extremely welcome. Now the stage was set for me to take my business to the next level, and I couldn't wait for the challenge!

LESSONS LEARNED FROM BEING AN AWARD-WINNER

Don't be shy - enter awards. My view on entering the HSBC Start-up Stars Awards was 'what have I got to lose?' This attitude served me well. I made great contacts and got free publicity, and that's why I went on to compete for many other award titles. Be optimistic. Put in for awards even if you think you are punching above your weight. For instance, entering a writing competition can only focus your mind, add to your productivity and may open doors you never knew existed.

Listen to your heart. When my old Assistant Chief spotted me in the newspaper and gave me a dressing down about How2Become I knew instantly that I was not going to let my business go, and I stood my ground. It's important to follow your instincts and hold on to your goals and dreams even when the going gets tough. You need to be resilient and dedicated. Don't let anyone else dictate your future.

Don't be afraid to ask. Some people thought I was cheeky to approach Sally Preston and quiz her about developing my business, but I was polite, and she could have politely turned me down if she wanted to. If you don't ask, you don't get. Be smart about who you seek advice from, however. Make sure you are dealing with an expert and not wasting time taking tips from amateurs.

Keep striving for more. I felt in my gut that How2Become was going to go from strength to strength and I recognised I needed to keep investing to build the business, and that I needed to get more savvy on the Internet. Never settle for second best. Keep giving one hundred percent and you will reap the rewards.

HAVE A MENTOR TO GUIDE YOU – YOU'LL ACHIEVE YOUR GOALS MUCH FASTER.

Richard McMunn

CHAPTER 8 –

Broadening my Horizons

After the positive experience I had with the HSBC Start-Up Stars Awards I had my eyes peeled all the time for similar opportunities. *Dragons' Den* seemed like an obvious prize to go for, and I put myself forward as a contender. I imagined that even if I didn't get any investment from the dragons, appearing on the show would be great free advertising for How2Become.

I passed the selection process, which I didn't find difficult. Having written so prolifically about job applications and how to get through interview stages, it would have been a pretty poor reflection on me if I couldn't pass a selection process like this myself! The next stage was to go in to the famous Den and film my pitch. The date was set and came round very quickly, probably before I'd really given enough thought to what I was letting myself in for.

Suddenly, I began to get cold feet and started wondering how this was going to go down with the Fire Service. I was still their employee, and featuring in the local paper hadn't been well received at all. Being on national TV was an ever bigger deal, so what sort of reaction would I get when my appearance on *Dragons' Den* was screened? I still felt no compunction to give up my career in the Fire Service, so why make life difficult for myself? I fretted right up until the day before filming. Part of me was thinking, 'just do it!' like I normally did, but I also had a bad feeling, and I didn't want to ignore my gut feeling.

Then, the night before filming, someone from *Dragons' Den* contacted me and asked me if I would show up in my firefighter's uniform. That made my mind up. I knew I'd be setting myself up for a heap of trouble if I did that and my instincts were telling me to avoid this situation. I immediately made my apologies and pulled out of the show and I felt relieved when I put the phone down. That's when I knew for sure I'd done the right thing.

After that I focused on pouring all my efforts in my free time into writing more books and building up the How2Become brand, as well as devising training courses. Sales were still extremely buoyant. Now, as well as clearing more than £3,000 a month from my job in the Fire Service, How2Become was giving me between £7,500 - £10,000 a month in additional income.

Over time, I invested in five properties. I knew now I wasn't going to stay in the Fire Service until I retired and that in leaving early my pension would take a hit, and I saw property investment as the next best thing to having a full Fire Service pension. I had already moved to Whitstable, renting out a house called 'The Boathouse' right on the sea front. I absolutely loved it down there, especially as there was a double garage for the Porsche and Yamaha motorbike I now owned. I can remember thinking back to the days when I was a spotty teenager, washing Marcel's Porsche 911, and now I had my own! The garage opened up onto the beach - I felt like James Bond! I was tasting the high life and enjoying the fruits of my labour, but I continued to work extremely hard and wrote more and more eBooks.

The band was doing well too. In 2007 the Sun newspaper ran a big article on tribute bands and Coolplay was one of just four bands mentioned. It was fantastic publicity for us and on the back of that we appeared in the NME and a few other magazines, and we got airtime on Virgin Radio and BBC Radio. In August that year the band played to a crowd of 40,000 at Hylands Park in Chelmsford, which is the V Festival site. Then we took booking for gigs in Crete, Portugal, Wales and Ireland – we were having a ball!

I was also enjoying my writing more than ever. One of the properties I bought was in Ambleside. I've always loved the Lake District and I used it as a place to write for a while, until I decided to rent it out. I loved the fact there were no distractions there, and I found myself being more productive than ever. My titles were starting to stack up, and I'd widened my list of books considerably.

Believe it or not, I still hadn't left the Fire Service! I was now working in fire safety at Canterbury. My title was Assistant Divisional Officer Fire Safety, a job I had also previously performed at Sittingbourne. I kept my head down at work and, as ever, still didn't really see the point in jacking in my job. I enjoyed the camaraderie of my colleagues, and I guess being in the Fire Service had become part of my way of life and identity, which put me off cutting ties. Immediately following that meeting with the Assistant Chief I had laid my cards on the table, officially writing to the Fire Service to declare my business interests and the fact I was selling insider information guides on how to pass selection processes for various jobs, including the Fire Service. I was completely transparent and made sure everything was clearly spelled out. The Fire Service never responded to that letter so I took it they accepted what I was doing.

When I moved to Canterbury I was delighted to find my bosses there had a completely different attitude to the Assistant Chief who'd given me the dressing down a couple of years earlier. They hadn't heard about the way I'd been reprimanded, and they clearly didn't think I was doing anything wrong, because they supported me.

'We love what you're doing on the Internet,' I was told enthusiastically. 'Can you review our website? It needs revamping.'

I agreed and put a lot of unpaid hours into reviewing their website with a view to creating a report on how it could be improved. My boss even included this task as part of my employment appraisal meeting, so as far as I was concerned, everything was fine!

At the same time I was working hard to put the finishing touches to my coaching courses, to mentor people in how to get into various jobs such as the Fire Service, the Police Service and the Ambulance Service. I charged £97 plus VAT for the day, and I invited people through the mailing list I'd built up. Once I got started I had about 20 people attending each one and I typically did a full day on both the Saturday and Sunday, going through interview questions and staging mock interviews. I enjoyed it, and the feedback I got was always very positive.

There was a big recruitment drive for firefighters in one of the large South Eastern Fire Services at the time, and lots of candidates who were applying for the jobs attended my courses and bought my book. Their success rate in securing jobs was sky high, so I was very pleased indeed. In fact, everything was going extremely well, and Coolplay was on a huge high too. Simon had been asked to do a big speaking gig at the O2 in London, and when he was figuring out how to make his presentation stand out against all the others, he hit on the idea of bringing the band on stage. It wasn't an easy fix but Simon had an answer to every potential problem. He simply wouldn't give up, even when logistical and technical issues seemed insurmountable and the organisers were telling him it would be impossible. The result of Simon's determination and persistence was that Coolplay got to perform to 8,000 people in one of the biggest venues in Europe!

I remember being backstage before the gig and feeling really nervous but also incredibly excited, all at the same time. This was such a big deal and I was thinking to myself, 'Just don't drop your bloody sticks!' If a guitarist hits a bum note during a song the chances are nobody will really notice, but it's different with drumming. If a drummer drops his sticks the whole song is ruined, so you can imagine how fraught my nerves were!

Going out on stage was the best feeling ever and seeing thousands of people sitting in the arena was amazing. For a few minutes, I imagined I was Chad Smith - one of my favourite drummers who plays with The Red Hot Chilli Peppers – and I imagined I was feeling exactly like he does when he plays to packed arenas all over the world. I could certainly do that for a living, I thought. It was absolutely brilliant, and a fantastic example of the truth that lies in that old saying 'if you don't ask you don't get'.

I had a real sense that my life was changing and I was moving in a different direction, and guess what? I wasn't wrong! I was on my way home from work one night when one of my superiors delivered some unexpected news which was to be the start of a life-changing situation.

'We're putting you on a stage three disciplinary.'

'Pardon? What for?'

'For selling the firefighter interview questions.'

I was informed by my boss that one of the South East Regional Fire Services had become suspicious when a large number of candidates gave the same answer to the interview questions they were asked. When they questioned this, the bosses got the same explanation again and again.

'I went on the firefighter recruitment course that bloke does in Kent. His training is excellent, and his book's so good!'

The Fire Service in question complained to Kent, and that is how I was now in the unpleasant position of being on a stage three disciplinary!

I went to see someone in HR I'd known for years and asked advice. I knew that a stage one disciplinary was for a minor misdemeanour. Stage two meant you were really in trouble, and stage three signalled that you were already half way out the door! It was serious, so what should I do now? My friend in HR explained that my bosses had no choice but to put me on a stage three. It was the correct and proper procedure given they believed I was 'selling' interview questions, which was a serious allegation. I can remember sitting at home thinking to myself how ridiculous this was. After all, I'd been totally open and honest with my employer and they'd even praised me during my latest appraisal for my business skills and were going to use these to revamp their website!

I was advised that I would have a month before I would face my disciplinary interview, and this gave me valuable time to think carefully what my next move was going to be. I certainly didn't want to be dismissed from the Fire Service. It was now 2009. I'd devoted nearly 17 years of my life to the job and was proud of everything I'd achieved. Ending my career by potentially being fired on a disciplinary was not going to happen. In my opinion it wasn't fair and it wasn't fitting. I had been writing my guides, under my own name, since 2004. Most importantly, I hadn't 'stolen' any material from the Fire Service. The interview questions I used in my guides and talks were my own personal suggestions, based on my many years of experience, and I had already been extremely upfront with my employer about everything I did with How2Become.

I had a few drinks that night in the Duke of Cumberland pub in Whitstable and made up my mind that I was going to resign from the Fire Service. It wasn't a difficult decision in the circumstances, and in any case, I'd been thinking about leaving more and more in recent times. I enjoyed the status the job gave me, and the camaraderie of my colleagues, but that was all that was keeping me there. I didn't need the money or the pension so it was silly, really. I should have left years before instead of working 18 hours a day as I had done for most of the precious five years, as I juggled my day job and the business.

I resigned the very next day, and when I walked away from the station I didn't look back. In fact, I was amazed at how quickly I forgot about the Fire Service; it was uncanny after so many years.

Not long after I resigned, I received a Certificate of Service from the Chief Fire Officer, congratulating me on completing 16 years and nine months of service. Along with the certificate I also received an invoice from the Fire Service for a missing fire glove! Apparently, I'd only returned one glove when I handed in my uniform, and I now owed the Fire Service the sum of £35. Unbelievable!

I thought about my old mentor Mick Brooker, and how he'd urged some of the other lads and me to go and live our lives to the full. I had felt a real sense of belonging to the Fire Service for so many years, but as soon as I left I realised it was all pretty shallow. I was dispensable. The loyalty and pride I'd felt for so many years was gone, in a flash. Now I was just me, Richard McMunn, entrepreneur.

I felt a little nervous and lonely, as I think a lot of people do when they leave a job after so many years' service. I'd lost a bit of my identity and my life was never going to be the same again, but I had no regrets. Now I could do what I'd wanted to do for a long time: be a full-time author and mentor. I was determined to make a success of it.

Interestingly, most of my friends in the Fire Service thought I was crazy.

'You've only got 13 years until you get your pension!' several said.

In fact, the rules were changing and in reality, I would have had to stay a lot longer.

Business people, on the other hand, we're very encouraging.

'About time too!' was a typical reaction.

I knew which camp I was in now, and I was looking forward to the challenges ahead.

LESSONS LEARNED FROM BROADENING MY HORIZONS

Don't be afraid to say no. I had a bad feeling about Dragons' Den and I pulled out, which is something I look back on with no regret at all. Be smart about the opportunities you take, and if your gut says a strong no, then you should definitely listen to it.

Exploit your skills. Devising a training course was an obvious next step for me, given the type of books I was writing and my background in training and giving presentations in the Fire Service. Ask yourself what skills you have in addition to being a writer and aspiring published author. How can you use them to boost your work as an author? Sometimes these skills are second nature and right under our noses, but we don't see them or realise their potential!

Keep your hobbies and interests going. I was very fortunate that Coolplay started to really take off just as my business was booming too. It's important to keep outside interests – your writing will benefit from the living you do outside of your office.

Don't believe your regular job defines you. I felt that no matter what, I'd always be a firefighter at heart and I'd always be tied to the Fire Service, like it was some kind of second family to me, and part of my identity. Big mistake! When I was gone, I was gone and soon forgotten. Follow your dreams and live your life to the full, because the company you work for ultimately will not miss you. Create your own identity!

DON'T BE AFRAID TO TAKE RISKS... IF YOU DO NOTHING, YOU GET NOTHING.

Richard McMunn

CHAPTER 9 –
Deciding to become a Published Author

Once I left the Fire Service I loved the freedom I had to decide exactly what I did with my working week and, with a lot more time on my hands, I wanted to get into publishing physical books. In fact, I'd been approached by one of the major publishing houses while I was still in the Fire Service, and I engaged with them because I thought it would be a great way for me to learn how the publishing process worked, so I could eventually do it myself.

After various meetings, I was offered a six-book deal, which probably sounds a lot more exciting than it actually was! I signed up, thinking I had nothing to lose and a lot of knowledge to gain. I already had most of the content as the books were going to be on how to get into careers I'd already written about, and I was looking forward to learning everything there was to know about publishing.

Unfortunately, I regretted signing up to the deal almost immediately. The publisher was paying me just £1,000 per book and the royalties were absolutely miniscule – I will tell you more about this in Chapter 11. But those factors turned out to be only part of the problem. I found I didn't like the cover designs the publisher came up with and the people I dealt with were incredibly slow at communicating with me, which I found extremely frustrating.

The six books eventually got published, but I wanted out of the book publishing deal pretty much soon after I had got into it! I felt the sales were too slow and I had lost control of the entire process. I like control, I like to get things done as quickly and efficiently as possible, and most importantly I realised I wanted to keep all the profits from my writing and not give them to a large publishing company! I don't think it's too much to ask when you're a hard-working, enthusiastic writer, do you?

The publishing house eventually allowed me to come out of the six contracts and I was now free to write and publish my own books on Amazon and in Waterstones. I was now a full-time writer and I was going to make it my mission to publish my own books, my own way.

I had no idea how much hard work this was going to be, but as ever I was very driven and incredibly determined to do my best and come out on top.

What follows in SECTION TWO is a detailed description of how to write and publish a bestselling book. You can read it chronologically or dip in and out of the chapters most relevant to you. At the end of the book, in SECTION THREE, I'll finish telling you my personal story and share some of the most valuable lessons I've learned over the years.

SECTION 2 –
How to Write and Publish a Bestselling Book!

CHAPTER 10 –
No Previous Experience Required

NO PREVIOUS EXPERIENCE REQUIRED

The reason I wanted to tell you about my life leading up to becoming a published author is because most of you who read this book will probably have no idea who I am, or the journey I have taken so far. I believe my story shows that ANYTHING is possible if you put your mind to it and work hard.

I have learnt throughout my life that if I apply discipline and structure to my work, I **WILL** be successful. Discipline is the root cause of my success. If you are disciplined and determined when writing and publishing your book, you will be successful!

As I've already explained, joining the Royal Navy was an extremely valuable experience for me, as it gave me responsibility, a trade, a sense of purpose and, most importantly, discipline. From the age of 16, I was required to conduct myself in a disciplined manner. This is something that I carried over into my next career as a firefighter, and then as an author.

Discipline is one of the main reasons for my success, and it will also be one of yours too. I will talk more about discipline as I progress through this guide, as it is something that you are going to have to take notice of when you start to write and publish your first book!

HOW DOES MY LIFE STORY IMPACT YOU?

I imagine some of you might be wondering why I decided to share my life story in so much detail in the first section of this book. Well, one of the reasons is that it takes much more than discipline (and hard work, of course) to become a published author. You also need to have an idea for the book that you intend to write. Most of us have lots of experience in life, which we can tap into and use when researching ideas for writing books. Whether it's by way of our qualifications, our career, hobbies and interests, or our passions, we all have something to write about.

As I've already described, my first book idea focused on what I was good at – teaching people how to get a job in the Fire Service. I'd risen through the ranks and had a vast amount of knowledge and experience that I could share. However, writing that first eBook was much more than a practical, logical step to take once I knew there would be a high demand for a book on how to become a firefighter.

Having the idea in the first place, and being more excited about it than I had been about my Fire Service career for many years, told me a great deal about where my passions lay and what I *really* wanted to do with my life. I learned that creating a business and pursuing my ambition of writing and publishing books was incredibly exciting to me, and in time it became a dream I simply had to follow because if I didn't, I knew I would not feel happy and fulfilled.

Having spoken to many aspiring authors over the years, many of them often tell me about their frustrations in their job, and how they do not find it fulfilling. I felt exactly the same when working in the Fire Service. Although it was a secure career and I was well paid it simply wasn't enough for me, or should I say it wasn't creative enough for me. As an author you will undoubtedly have a need and desire to be **creative** – this is what drives us forward, and is also what keeps us happy as individuals. I did not realise that I had this need until I started to write my first book.

Since the day when first I sat down in my cellar to write my very first book, I have gone on to author and publish over 150 books, many of which have become bestsellers. I'm immensely proud of this but, much more importantly, I have been very happy in my work as an author and publisher, and I have absolutely no regrets about leaving my day job.

As you know by now my first book idea came from a niche that I spotted whilst working in the Fire Service. Now, I want you to also think about the different experiences you have had in life so far, and how they might be used in order to write your first book. It's important to note that this applies to both non-fiction AND fiction.

When writing fiction, you'll often hear people telling you to 'write about what you know'. Although some people might be sceptical of this, and in some ways it's an overused cliché, there is a reason it's such a popular turn of phrase. Writing about something you know, is your chance to put your own individual spin on the subject. If you've ever tried to write about something completely alien to you – for example a city you've never visited, then you might have some idea of what I mean. It's really hard to write about something that you yourself don't know that well, and from my experience this lack of knowledge will detract from the writing. The better you know your subject, the better the quality of the prose will be.

Before we get into the different stages of the writing and publishing process, first let me give you my top tips for writing and publishing success.

CHAPTER 11 –

My Top 10 Tips For Writing And Publishing Success

MY TOP 10 TIPS FOR WRITING AND PUBLISHING SUCCESS

Within this chapter of the book, I have decided to list a number of insider tips and advice that will help you to achieve success when both writing and publishing books. These tips have helped me to continually achieve success in my publishing business, and I would like to share them with you. Although some of them may appear to be common sense, please take the time to read them and implement them during your writing and publishing strategy. Throughout this book, I'll expand on all of these points in greater detail, and give you some top tips for implementing them.

TIP 1 – DO NOT GET A BOOK PUBLISHING DEAL UNLESS YOU ARE THE NEXT JK ROWLING

Perhaps the main reason you are reading this book is because you are serious about publishing your own book yourself. This is great news! I can safely say that I am qualified to advise you here. The six-book publishing deal I described in Chapter 9 of SECTION ONE taught me a great deal. One of the main reasons why I pursued the contract in the first place was in order to learn the entire book publishing process myself. Of course, I did not disclose this to the publisher at the time, but it was my intention to learn the whole book publishing process, so that in the future I could do it myself and keep all of the profits in the process.

I can remember sitting in the plush London offices of the publishing company that I was trying to get a publishing contract with. They were very professional, and explained the entire process to me in detail. After reading my manuscripts, they informed me that they would need to get approval from their company Director before the draft publishing contracts would be sent over to me for consideration. At this point, I was informed about the royalty rate that I would receive from each book sold. After some tough negotiations, I managed to get myself 15% of net profits per book that was sold. To put it in simple terms, this effectively meant I would get approximately 30-50 pence for every book that was purchased. Now, call me ungrateful, but this did not sound fair at all. I was expected to write the content (60,000 words per book), and in exchange I would receive a fee of £1,000 per book and a royalty of just 15% net profit for printed book sales. On the train home, I considered the offer carefully. I managed to persuade myself that the contracts were worth more to me than the royalty rate, simply because I would get to learn the entire publishing process, which would eventually mean that I could do it myself. That's how I came to sign the deal but, as I've said before, unfortunately there were more hurdles ahead, ones I was not prepare to jump over! Disagreements over cover designs and the slow pace of communication were the main problems, leading me to ask to be released from the contract.

Here are the pros and cons of getting a standard book publishing deal:

Pros

- You do not have to put up any money in order to get your book published;

- The publisher **might** invest some money to promote your book;

- Your book **might** get stocked in Waterstones stores and WHSmith, although there are no guarantees;

- You will usually receive an advance of royalties.

Cons

- You will generally get a very low royalty rate (approx. 10%-15% of net profits);

- You may lose the rights to the work;

- You will be tied in to a contract for a very long time, effectively meaning you cannot sell your book anywhere else;

- You will lose control of the book cover design, title and the branding;

- As and when required, you will have to provide updates of your book to the publisher;

- The advance that you receive is exactly that, an advance. It will need to be earned against any royalties that your book generates, meaning you may never see a royalty cheque;

- The publishing contract can take a long time to get agreed, and negotiations can often be very frustrating. It took me many months to get approval for my book publishing contracts.

Hopefully you can now see the reasons why I encourage you to not get a book publishing deal, unless you are the next JK Rowling of course. In particular, moving away from the financial implications of a publishing deal, I think that creative control is a really big deal. Your book is a precious work of art, and therefore you deserve to have full input over key features such as the cover design and the title. It might even be the case that, if you are writing a fiction book, the publishing company wants you to make changes to the plot itself – in order to increase the book's commercial potential. Unless there is a genuine issue with the plot, then you shouldn't ever do this. Don't allow financial gain to impact upon your creativity. This brings me nicely onto my next point…

TIP 2 – DON'T BE IN IT FOR THE MONEY

Most people write and publish a book to make money. I fully appreciate that. However, whilst the financial rewards can be amazing, I advise that you put any ideas of financial reward to the back of your mind for the time being. The reason for this can be summed up in the following paragraph:

"When you write your first book, concentrate on writing chapters which your readers will find useful, enjoyable and impossible to put down. If you do this, the financial reward will come regardless."

Most people ask me how long it will take them to see a 5-figure monthly return from their writing efforts. My answer to this question is simple – if you focus solely on the financial return, then you probably won't see any profits at all. I then encourage them to focus on writing great content that will be of benefit to the reader, as this will have the following effect:

1. The reader will love the book, and they will then be more likely to leave a positive review on Amazon. If they do this, the book will sell more copies.

2. The more genuine 'verified' reviews your books receives, the better chance it will have of selling. If you write poor quality content, your book will almost definitely get criticised online.

3. Your readers will want to buy more of your books if the first one is great. This will also have the added benefit of giving your motivational levels a boost, something which is crucial to us as authors.

4. If you write great content then the chance of upselling in your book will greatly increase. For example, within my 'How2Become a Police Officer' book, I promote 1-day training courses on how to get into the Police Service. I can easily get 20 people to attend each course, all of whom have decided to purchase and attend my course after reading my book.

TIP 3 – HOW MANY PAGES SHOULD I WRITE?

Another common question that I get asked, is about how many pages a book should be. This is a very difficult to answer, as the answer is dependent on the genre/subject of the book, and also the type of reader and their needs. It will also depend on the pricing structure of the book, something which I will explain in greater detail during the next tip. However, when deciding on a rough page count for your book, consider the following:

- How long would the reader expect the book to be? If the book is relatively short, will the reader be disappointed, or conversely, if the book is overly long, will the reader feel overwhelmed?

- What is the page length of other books in the same genre?

- What would your printing costs be for your anticipated page length? The longer the book, the more expensive it will be to print!

There are many different factors to consider with page length, but let me leave you with one final tip: don't concentrate **too hard** on the page count. Just write your content until you feel you have created a fantastic book. This is particularly important if you are writing a fiction book. Of course, you still need to be disciplined, but on your initial draft, just write. Don't worry about how long the book is. The page count can be cut down during the editing stage, so focus on the really important stuff to begin with, and let the niggly sections come later.

Having said that, if you really do want me to give you a definitive page count to aim for, I suggest 150 to 250-pages for a non-fiction book, and 300-400> for a fiction book.

TIP 4 – HOW MUCH SHOULD I SELL MY BOOK FOR?

When it comes to pricing, the bottom line is this – if you price your book too cheaply then you won't make much money. On the other hand, if you price it too steep, you could put off potential customers. There are obviously higher production costs associated with physical books, whereas eBooks and Kindle books will give you financial reward far quicker.

Before you decide on how high to price your book, consider the following points:

1. Amazon will take up to 60% of the recommended retail price (RRP) of your printed book, depending on which programme you decide to sell your book through (more on this later during the relevant Amazon chapters). Understandably, most people are immediately put off by this. However, please read my Amazon chapters before dismissing Amazon as a marketplace from which to sell your work.

2. When you sell your book through the Amazon Kindle programme, you will be able to choose either a 70% or 35% royalty rate, depending on what price you decide to sell your book at. The level of royalty you choose will be mostly profit, as you will have no delivery or ongoing production costs. Choosing a 70% royalty rate means that you can price your Kindle book at a maximum of £9.99/$9.99, whereas the 30% royalty rate allows you to pick pretty much any price that you want.

3. With printed books, you will have to get them printed yourself, unless you decide to opt for the **Amazon KDP** programme (something I recommend you use). I choose to get my books printed through a third-party printer, and this method works very well for me, simply because I want to sell via multiple-channels and not just on Amazon. If I did want to sell solely on Amazon, then I would probably choose the KDP programme, to reduce my costs. It's worth noting that you can order printed copies of your book directly through your KDP account. However, the quality of the printed copies you receive might be lower than what an independent printer could offer you, and the cost will be higher too, so this is something to keep in mind.

4. The **unit price** per printed book will very much depend on the printer that you use. There are lots of printing companies out there vying for your business – the more you spend with them, the less it will cost you per book to get printed. Personally, I pay between £1 and £1.50 per 100 pages, but I do spend in excess of £100,000 per year with my chosen printer.

The vast majority of books that I sell will be launched with a RRP of between £12 and £15. I very rarely sell my books for less than this, simply because I aim to make at least £5 clear profit per book that I sell. For the books that I sell on my own website, I do not have to give anyone else the 60% margin, and therefore I will make a lot more profit per book sold via this marketplace. Because of this, it is within my interests to sell as many copies as I can via my own website. At the time of writing, I receive in excess of 100 transactions per day via my website.

The selling price will also be very much dependent on the genre of the book. For example, within my careers niche, I can realistically ask £12-£15 per book. This is because the reader will probably receive a salary of up to £30,000 per year, if they are successful after using my book. Therefore a £12-£15 investment is a reasonable exchange. However, if you are selling a novel or fiction printed book, then you may need to lower your price to the £10 mark or slightly lower. If it is a Kindle version, your price point will probably be lower still.

Before you decide on how to price your book, ask yourself the following questions:

1. How much will it cost me to get my physical book printed?

2. How much profit will I be left with per printed book, after costs?

3. What price point are other people within my genre selling their books at?

(This is a great strategy to use when considering the price of your book).

4. What price would I personally be willing to pay for a book of the same standard?

Having answered all the above questions, and taken into consideration all of the additional advice within this tip, you should be able to come up with a suitable recommended retail price for you book. Whatever happens, once you list your book at the RRP, you can always reduce it later on, if you find that it is not selling. Alternatively, you can always increase your prices if you feel it is too cheap.

TIP 5 – SERIOUSLY CONSIDER PUBLISHING A PRINTED BOOK

Most authors that I speak to believe the sale of printed books is on the decline – this is simply not true - they are actually on the rise. Although the sale of Kindle books is now outstripping that of printed books on Amazon, the sale of printed books is still growing. However, within certain niches I believe there will always be a strong demand for printed books. Whether or not you decide to opt for a printed book will very much depend on the genre of your book, and also the budget that you have at your disposal.

If you are writing and self-publishing a fiction novel or mystery, crime and thriller book, then I would advise you start off with a Kindle version. These genres of book tend to sell well in this format, simply because people like to read them whilst travelling on the train, plane or whilst on holiday. If you intend on publishing a book in either careers, business, finance, law, self-help, motivational, property, or business start-up, then you should seriously consider printed books, as they tend to sell better in this format. To give you an example, many of my printed books sell 5> times as many copies as they do on Kindle!

There are lots of benefits to publishing books on Kindle. Here they are:

- Relatively cheap to get published.

- Quick to publish through the Amazon Kindle Direct (KDP) Publishing website.

- High royalty rate (70% or 35%, depending on the pricing of your book).

- Huge demand for Kindle books in certain genres.

There are also a few downsides to publishing books on Kindle:

- Easier for customers to ask for a refund. The refund rate for Kindle books is higher than that of printed books.

- The perceived value of a Kindle book is lower than a printed book.

- A Kindle book will not reach places that a printed book can reach, and therefore the chance to upsell might be limited to just one reader.

And finally, here are the benefits to publishing books in Printed format:

- There are still many people who like the 'touch, feel and smell' of a printed book.

- A printed book is more likely to get passed around other readers, therefore increasing the opportunity for you to upsell to a wider audience. For example, I do know that most of my printed books are being used in schools and universities up and down the UK. This is great FREE promotion for my brand!

- For people running a business, a printed book is now seen as the 'new business card'. They are also great at generating leads for a business.

- As a published author, there is far more prestige attached to having your work published in physical/printed format.

- Printed books are a fantastic promotional tool when trying to upsell or promote additional products or services.

So, the choice of whether or not to publish your book in printed format is entirely down to you. However, my advice is to publish your book in both eBook (Kindle) format and print.

TIP 6 – GET YOUR BOOK COVER DESIGN RIGHT!

The first thing we are hit with when we enter a high street bookstore, is the mass of book spines sitting neatly on the bookshelves. These are placed deliberately, to grab the customers' attention. The book spine design and presentation were far more important in the pre-Amazon days. An example of this is the *Dummies Guides*. The next time you go into a Waterstones branch, take a look at all of the brightly coloured spines on the shelves, representing the many *Dummies Guides* on sale. The florescent colouring of their spines was an example of very clever marketing, in my opinion, simply because our eyes are drawn more to this colour than others. The design does a fantastic job of grabbing our attention.

Things have now changed, and we are buying more and more books online, through stores such as Amazon, Wordery and the Book Depository. Therefore, because of how books are presented online, the book spine has less significance during the buying process. What does have significance, is the actual front book cover itself – get this bit wrong and you will not sell many books, regardless of how good the content is! Later in this book, I have dedicated an entire chapter to creating quality book cover designs, and the kinds of things to consider when hiring a book cover designer. Read the chapter carefully, and follow the tips and guidance contained within it, to create truly awesome book cover designs.

TIP 7 – WORK HARD, PERSEVERE AND DON'T GIVE UP!

When you sit down to write your first book, it is understandably going to take up a lot of your time. Your evenings, weekends and every other spare minute will be needed to get your book completed, but the hard work and determination will be worth it.

When writing your book, you will probably find yourself, on occasions, feeling demotivated and lacking the desire to write. When this happens, stop writing. Take a break. Whilst I am no procrastinator, which is probably due to my military background, I do sometimes find it hard to write content. I have learnt not to get down or demotivated about the situation, and instead I simply take a few days off and come back to it when I am ready to.

It is very easy to burn yourself out as an author, and you will need to plan ahead to avoid this happening. This is why I encourage new authors and self-publishers to have a mentor – a mentor will be able to guide you and offer those all-important words of encouragement when they are most needed. Along with this, they'll also be able to provide you with crucial and honest feedback about your book. It's great to get an unbiased perspective on your work, as it's often hard for authors to spot the mistakes in their own writing.

When writing and publishing your book, you will need to have plenty of energy, so make sure you get adequate rest and exercise, and that you eat a healthy diet. You will no doubt have heard of the saying 'work hard, play hard'. Most successful authors and publishers know how to create a healthy work/lifestyle balance, and this is something that you should try to incorporate into your action plan very early on. Take time out to do things you like doing, and reward yourself when you reach significant milestones or chapters. When you do this, the feeling of success can become contagious.

Finally, like most people, I enjoy a few beers at weekends. However, I find that I am at my most productive when I cut out alcohol altogether. I have also noticed that when I cut out alcohol, my turnover and profits increase, simply because I get more done! When writing your book(s), I would urge you to consider your diet and alcohol intake – you need to have as much energy as possible when starting out, and all of these considerations will help.

Learn to take responsibility

Remember that you are the key to your destiny. You control your future, and therefore you must take responsibility for it. In order to become a successful author and self-publisher you don't have to be good at everything. Concentrate on coming up with book ideas and writing them; outsource everything else. I understand that in order to become successful I will need to hire people who are better than me at specific jobs or tasks – hence my love for outsourcing, which I will cover in greater detail during a later chapter.

TIP 8 – WORK TO AN ACTION PLAN

Another reason for my success is the fact that I work to a strict action plan. When I write a book, I always use the exact same action plan, which will consist of points such as:

- How many pages I will write every day.

- The type of research I will carry out.

- The proposed chapters of the book.

- When I intend on ordering the book cover artwork.

- The date I will put the book on Amazon 'pre-order'.

I get asked a lot of questions about how long it generally takes me to write a book. This very much depends on my enthusiasm levels, how excited I am about the book I am writing, and also whether or not the book is seasonal. What I mean by this is whether the book needs to be published and on sale for the busiest time of year for the book subject. For example, if you are writing fiction or a novel, then these books tend to sell very well in the build up to Christmas and during the school holidays. My career books always sell very well in January, when people are generally looking to make changes to their lives.

Let's assume you want to write a book which will consist of 100 pages. Within your action plan, I would recommend that you set out a minimum number of pages to write every day of the week. If you set out to write three pages every day, then you will have completed the book within a month. Writing three pages per day is something you can achieve, for sure!

TIP 9 – ENTER YOUR BOOK INTO AWARDS

Entering your book or publishing business into business awards can have a massive impact on the number of books that you sell. Apart from receiving free/invaluable publicity for your book, the recognition itself will drive you on to write more books.

For the first business awards that I entered – the HSBC Bank Start-Up Stars Awards - part of the initial entry process was to complete a short questionnaire. This asked me specific questions about my business and the books I was writing. As I mentioned in Chapter 7, just submitting the application form to enter the awards made me look at my business and business strategy in a different light. It didn't matter that I was not the overall winner. The publicity I received for taking part and being a South East regional winner was amazing. The coverage I got in local and national newspapers really gave my 'brand' a tremendous boost and really spurred me on to write more books.

The following year I was shortlisted in the National Online Recruitment Awards, and I then decided to enter awards specifically targeted at book publishers. I joined the Independent Publishers Guild (IPG) and entered their awards during the same year. Once again, by entering the awards, it made me focus on making improvements to my business.

I was shortlisted in the IPG's Publisher of the Year category as **Best Newcomer** the very first year I joined the organisation, and this gave me plenty of free publicity. This is what the judges said about my business at the time:

> *"How2Become is shortlisted on the back of rising print sales, downloads and web visits since launching. Judges admired the company's achievement on limited resources and its testimonials from grateful readers. "How2Become has performed well with decent margins — and is helping people to get jobs in difficult times."*

From the above comments made by the judges two words really stood out for me – "**helping people**". When writing books, I will **always** focus on writing high-quality content that is of benefit to the reader. These two words written by the judges just go to reaffirm this strategy – if you help people, the rewards will follow.

You can read more about this in SECTION THREE, where I continue the story of my transformation from writer into a prolific, award-winning published author. Also, at the end of SECTION TWO, I have provided a useful resources section which lists the book awards you may want to enter once you have published your own book.

TIP 10 – USE OUTSOURCERS

Some of the judges' comments that I referred to in the previous tip were in relation to my achievements on "limited resources." What they basically meant was the fact that I have achieved so much without employing lots of people. Again, fast forward a few years, and I've now got ten members of staff working for me. This isn't a huge number by any means, but it's a sign of fantastic growth nonetheless. Sometimes you don't need enormous numbers of people in order to do an amazing job, and the reason for this, is outsourcers.

Outsourcing is the practise of hiring others to carry out work that you are either not good at, or that you don't have the time to do. Or, my preferred description of outsourcing is this:

To obtain a professional service from an external expert, in order to MASSIVELY increase the profits in your book writing and publishing business!

I consistently generate six-figure net profits every year, and this is largely because I outsource effectively.

When people start a business, they generally find themselves doing everything. This was certainly the case for me when I first started out. I can remember doing literally **EVERYTHING** in the beginning, such as answering the customer service emails, learning how to build the website from which I was going to sell my books, writing my books, and also sending out the books to my customers. As time went on, I learnt more about the art of outsourcing, and how it could free up more time for me to work 'on' my publishing business as opposed to working 'in' it.

I generally work on the 80/20 principle, which effectively means that in my life there are certain activities that I do (my 20%) which account for the majority (my 80%) of my happiness and my output. My 20% consists of the following:

• I keep fit.

• I eat healthily.

• I only DO things that I am good at (write books and mentor authors)

I then outsource the rest!

My advice to you as an aspiring author is to only work on the things that you are good at, and that will probably only mean writing the content for your books. For example, it is very important for my publishing business, How2Become.com, that we actually write the books and present the online training videos. After all, it is How2Become's skill and expertise in recruitment that people are paying for, therefore it would not make sense if we outsourced these elements of the business. Here's a full list of things that I outsource in my publishing business:

o   I outsource my website design/development.

o   I outsource my book cover design and branding.

o   I outsource my proofreading/editing.

o   I outsource my printing.

o   I outsource my customer service/care.

o   I outsource my eBook conversion.

o   I outsource my website sales-copy.

o   I outsource my online advertising/marketing strategy.

o   I outsource my social media marketing.

Before you employ someone in any business, you should ask yourself the following questions:

Q1. Do I really need to employ this person?

Q2. Are there alternatives, such as using outsourcers?

If you can outsource the work, then I would strongly encourage you to do so.

During one of the later chapters I will go into more detail about the art of outsourcing, and how it will help you to self-publish your book(s).

CHAPTER 12 –
Researching Ideas For Book Subjects

The planning stage of writing your book is one of the most important aspects to your success. I consider this to be an integral part of my publishing strategy. By carrying out effective research, I am able to pretty much determine whether or not a book will become a success, even before I have started writing it. Most authors start writing their book without carrying out any research. Thus, they are unable to ascertain whether or not it has a chance of selling. I believe this is a big mistake. If you carry out little or no research prior to writing your book, then you will soon become demotivated, once you realise that it hasn't sold as many copies as you hoped it would. This will then have the knock-on effect of draining all of the drive and enthusiasm required to write further books.

PLANNING AND FICTION

The above advice applies to both fiction and non-fiction. You might think that research and fiction don't exactly go hand-in-hand, but this is incorrect. Even fiction writers need to conduct thorough research of the locations that they are writing about. Here's a secret that I'm pretty sure most fiction writers don't actually do – when writing a fiction book, **you need to research your own characters.** What do I mean by this? Allow me to explain.

Let's say you sit down to write a fiction novel. You might have several characters in mind who you want to put in your book. My question is, how well do you know these characters? Do you know them, or do you really know them? The difference between **knowing** and **understanding** your characters is crucial in my opinion. Let me show you the difference:

A writer who *knows* their characters:

- Knows their motivations, goals and narrative objectives.

- Knows their love interest.

- Knows their family history.

- Knows what they look like.

- Knows how they will progress in the novel.

In contrast, a writer who *understands* their characters:

- Understands their motivations, goals and narrative objectives, as well as their external objectives (objectives not related to the narrative of the book).

- Understands their love interest, their romantic history, writes the way that they interact with their love interest in a way that corresponds with their romantic history, past partners, etc.

- Understands their family history, their relationship with certain family members, where they grew up, where they went to school, who their friends were at school, who their best friend was growing up.

- Understands their favourite food, drink (the brand for example), colour, what things they associate with this colour, etc.

Need I say more? Essentially, what I'm trying to get at here is that you need to make an enormous effort to write up everything that you possibly can about your characters. The best novels are the best, because the characters in those novels act in a way that is consistent with unspoken history. That is to say, the writer has thought of an entire backstory for this character, and personality, and then written a character whose actions and behaviours correspond with this. And the best part of this is – you don't even have to give this part to the reader. It's for you to use as an outline, so make sure you plan your own characters beforehand. This will make them far easier to write.

THE FIRST STEPS

To help you get off to the right start with any book-writing venture, take a look at the following important steps:

STEP 1 – CHOOSING A GENRE

The first step in writing your book is to select a genre. Whilst there are many different book genres out there, I recommend you choose one which:

- You are passionate about;

- You have a desire to write in;

- You have knowledge or expertise of;

- There is demand for.

I recommend you choose your genre from the list of categories listed on Amazon, purely because this is the place you will sell the vast majority of your books – more about Amazon in later chapters.

At the time of writing, the following book categories are listed on Amazon:

- Antiquarian, Rare & Collectable

- Art, Architecture & Photography

- Biography

- Business, Finance & Law

- Calendars, Diaries & Annuals

- Children's Books
- Comics & Graphic Novels
- Computing & Internet
- Crime, Thrillers & Mystery
- Education Studies & Teaching
- Fiction
- Food & Drink
- Gay & Lesbian
- Health, Family & Lifestyle
- History
- Home & Garden
- Horror
- Humour
- Languages
- Mind, Body & Spirit
- Music, Stage & Screen
- Poetry, Drama & Criticism
- Reference
- Religion & Spirituality
- Romance
- School Books
- Science & Nature
- Science Fiction & Fantasy
- Scientific, Technical & Medical
- Society, Politics & Philosophy
- Sports, Hobbies & Games
- Travel & Holiday
- Young Adult

Believe it or not, my 'How2Become' career books fall under the 'Business, Finance and Law' category on Amazon.

Which is the biggest genre?

Unsurprisingly, of the people who buy at least one book a year, 8 out of 10 buy a fiction book. The best-selling fiction books are mystery, crime and thriller. Now, I am not saying that you should go away and start writing a book in the fiction category, far from it. What I am saying, though, is that it is worth carrying out some research into the level of demand that your chosen genre falls into.

My niche 'career books' genre is actually a very small market with regards to demand, yet I have still managed to make over £6,000,000 from it so far. On the flipside, **Erotic Fiction** is one of the largest book markets on Amazon, yet it is discreetly hidden from the homepage. When you get time, type 'erotic fiction' into the Amazon search bar on the homepage and take a look at the rankings of some of the books in this category!

Applying Maslow's Hierarchy of Needs to book research

During my research I will more often than not use Maslow's Hierarchy of Needs. Maslow wanted to understand what motivates people. He believed that individuals possess a set of motivation systems, unrelated to rewards or unconscious desires. Maslow stated that people are motivated to achieve certain needs. When one need is fulfilled, a person seeks to fulfil the next one, and so on. When I think of a potential book subject, I will always ask myself the following question - "Is there demand for my book based on Maslow's triangle of needs?" Although this method of research does not guarantee that a book will sell, it does give me the confidence that my book has a better chance of selling, as it falls into a category which defines the basic requirement of people's everyday needs.

To demonstrate how effective Maslow's triangle is, Facebook sits slap bang in the '**LOVE AND BELONGING**' section of the triangle. During the early years of Facebook, many people were surprised at its success. However, if we study Maslow's Hierarchy of Needs we can see that a 'sense of connection' is a <u>must</u> to ALL human beings. This is exactly the reason why we feel a sense of connection when people 'LIKE' a photograph we have posted on our Facebook page.

In order to explain the process, below I have listed which genre of books fall into which level of Maslow's triangle.

Maslow's Hierarchy of Needs

Self-actualization	Self-development books Continuous development books
Self-esteem	Motivational books & self-help books Building confidence books
Love and belonging	Relationship books, novels and fiction
Safety and security	Money management books Property books Career books, fitness and health books
Psysiological needs	Survival books & cooking-related books

So, once you have chosen the genre or title for your book, take a quick look at Maslow's triangle to see whether or not it fits into one or more of the Maslow needs.

Of course, there are many authors out there reading this book who will already have an idea for a book subject. For those of you who are in this position, I still recommend that you carry out the **researching steps** within this chapter, in order to ascertain whether or not your book will sell.

STEP 2 – CHOOSING A BOOK SUBJECT IDEA

Once you have chosen your book genre, it is now time to choose the actual **subject** for your book.

One of the most effective ways to choose a book subject is to use my BOOK IDEAS GENERATION FORM. The form was created very near to the start of my career as an author, when I noticed a pattern to the ideas that I was generating. The form is shown below, and is immediately followed by an explanation for each section of the form.

Richard McMunn's Book Ideas Generation Form

QUESTIONS	ANSWERS	BOOK IDEA
What qualifications do I have?		
What am I good at?		
What courses have I been on during my life?		
Have people ever asked me for help or advice?		
What am I passionate about?		
Have I ever won any awards?		
What do my friends or relatives know that could help me?		

I have used this form to great effect over the last few years, in order to generate book ideas, and I am certain it will help you too. I have also used it on numerous occasions to help my students come up with book ideas, via my one-to-one author mentoring and coaching programme. To demonstrate how I have used the form over the years, I will provide you with my answers to the questions, and also the book ideas that I generated from those answers.

QUESTIONS	ANSWERS	BOOK IDEA
What qualifications do I have?	3 x GCSEs	How to become a millionaire with poor exam qualifications!
What am I good at doing?	Coaching others to write and publish books.	This book.
What courses have I been on during my life?	Search Engine Optimization training courses.	SEO for business owners.
Do people ever ask me for help or advice?	How to join the Fire Service. How to promote their business on YouTube.	My 'How2Become a firefighter' book. How to promote a business on YouTube.
What am I passionate about?	Helping others to achieve success.	This book and all my 'How2Become' series books.
Have I ever won any awards?	Numerous business awards. Nielsen Digital Marketing Award Winner.	How to become an award-winning business. How to promote a book to become a bestseller.
What do my friends or relatives know that could help me?	My father was a magistrate.	How2Become a magistrate (Number 1 bestseller).

You will notice from my answers that I am never short of book ideas. One question that should open lots of doors for you, is the final one – "What do my friends or relatives know that could help me?" When completing the form, it dawned on me that my father was a magistrate. Therefore, he was a source of information that I could potentially tap into, in order to help me to write a book on this subject. Whilst he would not disclose any information regarding how to pass the selection process, he was able to tell me key facts about the role and the type of qualities and attributes needed to become a competent magistrate. After using his information and carrying out further research, I created a number 1, bestselling book entitled *How To Become a Magistrate*.

Using the newspapers and online media to generate niche book ideas

Newspapers and online news websites are a great source of information for identifying niche book ideas. A few times a week, I will spend at least 30 minutes in my local Costa Coffee reading the papers and searching for ideas from which to write new books. Here's an example of a book idea I spotted in **The Telegraph** one day:

HEADLINE: British Airways to recruit 800 pilots!

As soon as I saw this headline, I knew it was a great opportunity to write a book entitled 'How to Become an Airline Pilot'. If British airways needed to recruit 800 pilots, then the competition for these jobs would be huge! I also figured that if British Airways needed to recruit *that* many pilots, other airlines would probably soon follow suit. There was just one problem; I had absolutely no idea of how to become a pilot!

Using my 'can-do' attitude, I sat there in the coffee shop, thinking of ways to find an airline pilot who could either help me to write the book, or write it for me with a view to sharing the royalties. After a few minutes searching online, I found a forum for pilots online. I then registered as a user and simply posted a message on their forum, asking if there were any pilots available to help me write a book on this subject. Soon after posting the message, I had found myself a pilot, and we arranged to meet up to discuss how he could help me to write the book. Again, this book ended up becoming a bestseller on Amazon. I can spot book niche ideas every single day of the week, and I can confidently say that I will never run out of ideas – the only problem is having enough time in the day to write them all.

Once you follow my methods and strategies for generating exciting and niche book ideas, I can assure you that will never run out of them.

Book subjects to avoid

Whilst there is a market out there for most book subjects, you do need to be careful not to fall into the trap of writing a book where the competition is unhelpfully fierce, or where the market is oversaturated. Through trial and error, I have learnt over the years that books will sell far better if they are targeted towards a particular niche section of individuals or groups. Don't just assume that your book will sell thousands of copies, just because it's in a popular category. Consider niche areas of your chosen book first, as these are far more likely to sell better, and provide you with a sustainable future as an author. An example of this would be in relation to a fitness book. There are so many books available on fitness that you would be hard pushed to ever make any money at all from a book that simply covers 'general' fitness. However, if you choose a niche area of the fitness genre – fitness for pregnant women or the over 50's for example – it will have a better chance of selling.

STEP 3 – HOW MANY PEOPLE ARE SEARCHING FOR YOUR BOOK SUBJECT ONLINE?

Once you have come up with your book subject idea, you now need to take the time to see whether or not there is a market for it. To achieve this, I recommend that you use the GOOGLE KEYWORD PLANNER TOOL. To find this tool, simply type **'Google Keyword Planner Tool'** into the Google search bar.

To get access to the tool, you'll need to create a Google AdWords account. When you set up your account and login, select the 'Tools' drop-down menu option, followed by 'Keyword Planner'.

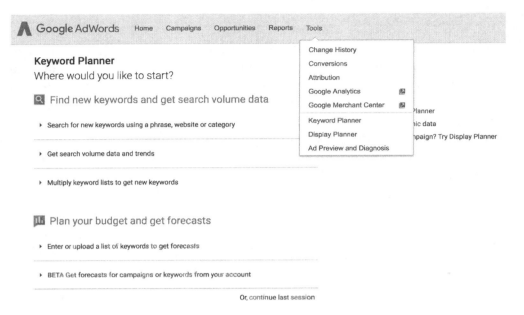

As authors who are researching what people are searching for on the web, we need to select '**Search for new keywords and using a phrase, website or category**'. Selecting this option will enable us to perform normal keyword research, where we simply enter our **book idea keywords**, and Google will then show us the searches that people are making, based on your keywords. The basic premise of this strategy is to determine whether or not people are searching for information based on our book subject. If they are, then there is a good chance that your book will sell.

In the following image, which forms part of the Google Keyword Planner, you will be able to enter keywords and phrases based on your book subject idea(s). Once you have entered your keywords and phrases, simply click '**GET IDEAS**', and Google will tell you what people are searching for on Google, how many (approximately) searches there are, and also whether the competition is HIGH or LOW with regards to people advertising on Google through AdWords.

> **NOTE: Through research, I have found that if people are searching for a specific area of information on Google, they will also be searching for it on Amazon, too.**

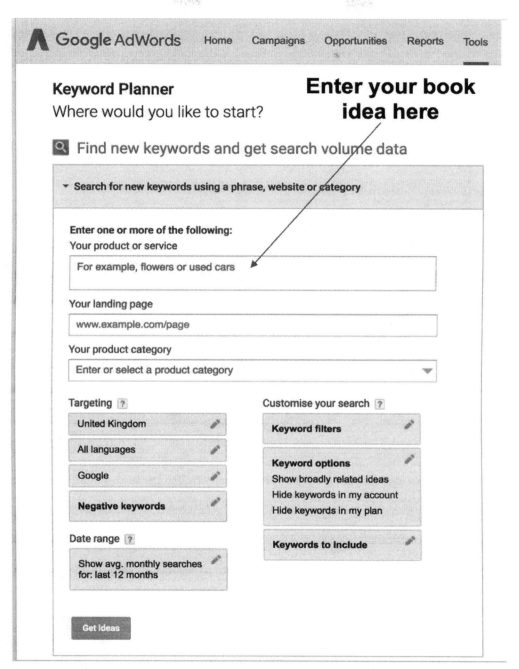

As an example, when I was researching my *How to Become a Pilot* book I found there to be 8,100 searches online every month with LOW competition. This immediately informed me that there was a potential gap in the market.

You will see from the results below that there are 8,100 average monthly searches for 'how to become a pilot' with LOW competition on AdWords. Although this LOW indicator does not mean there is LOW competition with regards to your book subject, it does mean there is LOW competition with regards to Google AdWords, which is something you may decide to use in order to promote your book online.

Results of Google searches based on the keyword phrase 'how to become a pilot'.

Find keywords   Review plan

Ad group ideas	Keyword ideas		
			Shc
Keyword (by relevance)		**Avg. monthly searches** [?]	**Competition** [?]
how to become a pilot	⌇	8,100	Low

Please note: for those authors who are writing fiction books in genres such as mystery, crime and thriller etc., the Google Keyword Planner tool may not be much use to you, as your book title will be very different to the ones that I personally create and search for. However, what is reassuring to know is that there are huge levels of search traffic on Amazon for your particular genre of book.

STEP 4 – GO TO AMAZON AND ASSESS THE COMPETITION

Step 4 in the research process is to go to Amazon, and type the same book subject idea into the search bar near the top of the homepage. Prior to publishing the book on How to Become a Pilot, I found there to be no competitors. If you go to Amazon.co.uk right now and type in 'how to become a pilot' you should see my book sitting near the top spot in the search results. The reason why it is there is because it sells well, and it also matches the keyword phrase that you have typed into Amazon. Hopefully you can now see how effective my research strategy is, and also how effective the Google Keyword Planner is.

What if there is lots of competition for the book subject?

If you go to Amazon, and find that there are many other books titled the same as your proposed book, do not be put off. Before you change subject, consider the following:

- If the competitor's book has poor reviews, this is an opportunity for you to create a better quality book.

- If the book cover design is sub-standard, this is an opportunity for you to create a better quality book.

As mentioned, I will be covering book cover design in detail in a later chapter, and will show you about how important a book cover is to your overall book publishing strategy and success.

An example of how I beat the competition!

I think it would be useful for me to provide you with an example of a competitor's book that I found on Amazon, which I felt I could drastically improve on. I had carried out some research using the Google Keyword Planner tool and found there to be nearly 15,000 monthly searches for 'Armed Forces Tests'. Because I sell books based on careers within the Armed Forces, I decided that I wanted to create a testing book that provided the reader with sample Armed Forces Tests. Unfortunately, when I followed step 4 of my strategy, I found there to be a competitor's book selling tests on the same subject.

The competitor's book was very well established, and had been selling strongly in the bestsellers list for some time. Despite this, I suspected there were a number of perceived flaws with this particular book. To begin with, I felt the book cover did not do the content of the book justice. Also, the publisher had decided to call the book *Practice tests for the Armed Forces*. When I returned to the Google Keyword Planner tool, I found that there were ZERO monthly searches for this phrase. These two flaws, as I perceived them to be, gave me the confidence to create my own book on this subject. Here's what I did next:

1. I created a book that included more sample tests. In total, my book contained an additional 50 pages worth of tests than my competitors.

2. I improved the book cover to make it look both simple and professional.

3. I titled my book exactly what people were searching for – **ARMED FORCES TESTS** (approximately 15,000 monthly searches at the time).

4. I increased the price of my book by £5!

The reason why I increased the price of my book is because I am a genuine believer that in order to compete with another business, you do not necessarily have to compete with them on the price. There are many people out there who will pay a premium for a book, product or service, if they know they are going to get a better standard product or service.

My strategy worked, as I started to sell a lot more than my competitor's book – after a few months competing with me they decided to stop publishing their book.

MY ARMED FORCES TESTS BOOK COVER

THE TESTING SERIES

Richard McMunn

ARMED FORCES TESTS

Sample test questions for the RAF, Royal Navy and Army recruitment tests

THE **TESTING** SERIES

You will notice that the above book cover design is clear, simple and the title does exactly what it says on the tin – something which I think is very important for a non-fiction type book. If you head over to Amazon.co.uk and search for **Armed Forces Tests**, you will see my book appear near the top of the search results. Those eagle-eyed authors amongst you will also notice I have published two books under the same title! Why have I done this, you might be asking? The answer is simple – to dominate the niche. There is nothing to stop you from writing two books on the same topic. Yes, you will have to write new content and a create a new cover for the second book, but there are no rules that say you are not allowed to compete with yourself in a niche or subject area.

If you have read this chapter, implemented my strategies, and still cannot come up with an idea for a book, I recommend that you attend one of my 1-day book writing and publishing courses and I will help you come up with a book idea. You can find out more about my courses at:

www.BookPublishingCourses.com

CHAPTER 13 –

Creating An Action Plan And Writing Your Book

CREATING AN ACTION PLAN AND WRITING YOUR BOOK

In this chapter I will explain the process that I go through when writing my books, including the action plan that I follow. Whilst I will also provide advice on chapters and the style of writing for various genres, your own style of writing is what will make your book unique. The way in which I write is not perfect, far from it, yet it is ideal for the genre of books I write. I have had no formal training or coaching with regards to my writing style, as I want it to be as natural as possible and from the heart. So, the first piece of advice that I want to give you in this chapter is to simply write in your own style and from the heart. It is this approach that will make your book unique. When it comes to the proofreading and editing stage, this is where any mistakes or errors will get identified and amended.

The action plan

Having an action plan will allow you to keep on track and get your book finished. Within this chapter I have provided you with a copy of the exact action plan I have used many times over the years to write and publish bestselling books.

Before putting pen to paper, or fingers to keyboard, you should decide roughly how many pages you are going to write each day. My advice is to start off small, and gradually build up, as you feel your enthusiasm levels increasing and as your book starts to take shape. 300-400 words per day are sufficient in the beginning. John Grisham, one of the world's most successful authors, started his career as a lawyer. He used to get up very early every morning before work, and write just one page.

Before you start writing your book, you should have an outline of what the book will include. Personally, I write down all the proposed chapter titles on one page, and then start to write the content for each one as and when I feel enthused. What's more, I do not necessarily always complete the chapters in chronological order. For example, when writing this book, I completed the chapter on OUTSOURCING first, as this is a subject I feel very enthusiastic about. I knew that once I had completed this chapter the rest would fall into shape.

The bottom line is there are no rules when it comes to writing a book – be creative and feel free to experiment. For my very first book, *How to Become a Firefighter,* I decided to include a chapter called **MY TOP 10 TIPS FOR SUCCESS**. This chapter has now featured in over 75% of my books, as my readers tell me it is one of the most useful sections.

When and where should you write?

I personally like to write at the end of the day, usually in the evening – I find that I am at my most creative and productive during this time, and I am often still writing late into the night and through to the early hours. At the time of writing this chapter it is 2.35am on a Friday morning! Only you will know what time is best for you to write at. Like John Grisham, you may find that you write more effectively very early in the morning, before you go off to work. Take the time to think about the time of day you feel you would be best suited to writing, and then allocate this time into your schedule. Top tip though, if you are struggling with ideas or motivation, don't be scared to try and change up both your timing, and your location. For many people, a change of scenery can be exactly what they need to get some fresh new ideas, and start filling up the pages with great content.

Some people like to write in bulk, and I can fully understand why they find this method stimulating. By writing in bulk I actually mean taking a few days or even a week out of their schedule, and then blitzing the book in one go. This can sometimes be a useful strategy. As I also discuss in SECTION THREE, from the money I have made through writing books, I decided to buy a property in the Lake District, one of my all-time favourite locations. One of the reasons I bought this property is so that I had somewhere to go off and write whenever I felt the urge to. There are no distractions in the Lake District, and for me this is a great place to write.

If you have a family, then I would recommend telling them that you are going to write a book. They will be able to encourage you and motivate you, and they will also hopefully give you some peace and quiet when you need it, so that you can concentrate on your writing. Furthermore, you can consult them for a quick proofread every now and then!

Get feedback along the way

During my book writing and publishing training courses, I encourage all authors to seek feedback after they have completed each chapter. In fact, for those authors who are on my author mentoring programme, I review the content for them!

There is nothing worse than writing a book and then having to rewrite it, just because you didn't let anyone look at it. Have a mentor on hand to help you throughout the writing process. One other thing with regards to feedback – have thick skin! As an author you are putting your work out there to be read and reviewed. I can remember getting my first negative review on Amazon, and to be honest it really upset me. After a few days feeling sorry for myself I decided to turn the negative review into a positive situation. I engaged with the reviewer on Amazon and asked him to help me improve the book. He provided me with some tips on how he felt the book could be improved, and I took his comments on board when writing the updated version. Nowadays I advise authors not to communicate with reviewers who leave negative reviews. Instead, I recommend you ask yourself if the review is accurate and whether or not you could improve your book for the next print run or publication.

In the past I've taken part in writing seminars/workshops where my work has been absolutely shredded by the group. This is a brutal experience, but my belief is that it genuinely makes you stronger. The reality is that writing is a personal act. You are opening up yourself to people's views and opinions, and even though sometimes these can be hard to take, always remember that every piece of constructive criticism is worthwhile. The opinions of others do matter – because at the end of the day, they are your audience and your readership.

Learn to hate procrastination

Procrastination is the action of delaying or postponing something – or in this case putting off writing your book. As authors we need to avoid this as much as possible. If you are the type of person who is likely to procrastinate, then get yourself a mentor, or at least someone who will push and nag you to get your book completed – accountability is king!

I have never had a problem with procrastination, but I can understand why people do it. You just have to keep going. If you follow an action plan and stick it somewhere prominent, like on your fridge door, then you are far more likely to succeed. I usually find that once I have written three chapters of my book, my motivation levels increase. At this stage I feel like I am making good progress, and once you get past the halfway stage, then the finishing line is in sight. Just keep focusing on seeing your book on sale in Waterstones and on Amazon, and visualise the book flying off the shelves.

For those who want to write a novel

The first step when preparing to write a novel is to think about the types of book that you really love. Don't try to write a story about something that you think your friends or family will love. Instead, write about what gets <u>you</u> going and what you are passionate about. You see, if you write about what you are passionate about, then it will be easier to write from the heart. The writing will be better, and the book will sell better. We are aiming to make your writing a pleasurable and 'easy' experience. A great way to test what you are passionate about would be to write down a list of five things that you are crazy about in your life. For me I just love helping people, which is why I enjoy writing career/self-help books that make a difference to others' lives. Write down your list of five crazy obsessions, and see if it doesn't inspire you to write.

The 'character'

I've already said a little bit about planning your characters, but I cannot emphasise how important it is to get this right. When writing a novel, you need to carefully consider the main character. You need to live with the character and learn to love them. You should also consider making your character flawed in some manner. People love to read about exciting and unique characters, as it takes them away from everyday life. You have to make your reader not want to put down the book. You should also not be afraid to write in extremes. Take your character to places they wouldn't normally go, and allow them to do things they shouldn't be doing. Do not be afraid to experiment with scenarios and situations within your book, and try to be edgy. You can always take out parts or sections of the book later on if need be. If you do this, you will maintain your reader's attention and enthusiasm.

Once you have decided on your character and his or her flaws, start your novel by writing a few lines with any of following beginnings, and then just see where it takes you:

"I have something to tell you and I don't think you are going to like it…"

"I have kept a secret for the last ten years and I can no longer keep hold of it…"

"On the surface he was every woman's dream; however…,"

"I have never told anyone this before…"

Of course, you can come up with your own beginnings for your novel, but I am sure you will find the above exercise helpful in getting started.

Your character has to have something going on in their life that is compelling. A great way to come up with this is to think about your friends and family. Do any of them have compelling problems, either now or in the past, that have caused major issues or problems? If so, you may decide to base your character on them without actually telling them. At the heart of every great story is usually a conflict or major issue – you should decide what that issue is before you start writing. The issue or problem should be close to your character throughout the book.

A great tip for writing novels is to ask yourself whether or not the storyline is believable. Even if you introduce ghosts and fairies, you can still make the story believable via the style of writing you adopt. Above all else though, remember that the novel is *your* book and nobody else's, therefore you can write it however you like.

The structure of your book

Book structure is dependent on the genre of the book that you are writing. There are no hard and fast rules that you must follow, only guidelines. The general structure I use for my genre of book is as follows:

Title page – on this page I will include the main title of my book, the strapline, my company logo and the authors name.

Copyright and ordering information page – on this page I will always include my copyright notice and details of how people can order my books. It usually takes the following format:

Orders: Please contact How2Become Ltd, Suite 14, 50 Churchill Square Business Centre, Kings Hill, Kent ME19 4YU. You can also order via the email address info@How2Become.co.uk.

ISBN: INSERT YOUR 13-DIGIT ISBN HERE

First published in 2018 by How2Become Ltd.

Copyright © 2018 Richard McMunn. All rights reserved.

All rights reserved. Apart from any permitted use under UK copyright law no part of this publication may be reproduced or transmitted in any form or by any means, electronic or mechanical, including photocopying, recording, or any information, storage or retrieval system without permission in writing from the publisher or under licence from the Copyright Licensing Agency Limited. Further details of such licenses (for reprographic reproduction) may be obtained from the Copyright Licensing Agency Ltd, Saffron House, 6-10 Kirby Street, London EC1N 8TS.

NOTE: If you would like a copy of my book templates and copyright notices to use within your own book, you can download them at AuthorToolkit.co.uk

It is also good practice to include the name of the company which has printed your book on this page. Printing companies often have a tough time within the industry, and it is recognised as good practice to promote them.

Foreword

Whilst a foreword is not a necessity, it can provide a useful 'lead in' to the main content of your book. The foreword will normally be written by someone of importance – perhaps a person in a position of authority.

The aim of the person writing the foreword is to introduce an author/work to the world, which can be accomplished in a variety of ways. The person writing the foreword could either write about a specific chapter in the book, the book as a whole (assuming they have read it), or the author's work in general. If they know the author personally, then it is advisable that they talk about this relationship. If they don't, they could instead discuss how the author's work has affected their life or the importance of the work they are introducing.

If the person is writing a foreword to introduce a new edition of a book, it is advisable that they talk about what's different in the current edition.

To help you, here is a sample foreword written by someone in a position of authority and expertise. This foreword was written for an author who I coached as part of my VIP author mentoring programme. His book, entitled How to Become a Driving Instructor, is available to view on Amazon.

Sample foreword

ABOUT BILL LAVENDER

Foreword by Robin Cummins OBE former DSA Chief Driving Examiner

This guide has been written by industry insider, Bill Lavender. Well known for his "Better Training" features in adiNEWS for the last ten years, Bill became an Approved Driving Instructor in 1982 and has spent most of his career at the British School of Motoring (BSM) in various senior training and development roles, including NVQ and BTEC awards for instructors. He was also responsible for the company's learning resources, including retail products for learner drivers.

Bill now works freelance as an independent road safety consultant, specialising not only in driving instructor Continuing Professional Development (CPD), but also delivering Driver Certificate of Professional Competence (dCPC) courses for professional bus and lorry drivers. By producing this guide, Bill has reflected on his extensive knowledge and experience of the industry to provide first-hand guidance for anyone who is thinking about becoming an Approved Driving Instructor (ADI). Being a driving instructor is a very rewarding career for the right person. New learner drivers rely on good instructors who are suited to the job to not only prepare them to pass their tests first time, but also to help them enjoy the experience of learning how to stay safe on our busy roads.

The difference between the number of people first registering with the DSA to become an ADI and the number actually qualifying is a concern. There are clearly many people who must be very disappointed that they have not been able to qualify or have not been able to make a living out of the business for one reason or another.

It is important that every new potential instructor knows exactly what to expect from the industry, who is there to help you, and the best way to ensure that all expectations are fully met. As well as important technical information such as the lesson plans, you will find good advice on what it takes to be a successful instructor. There are many attractions to the job, and how well you do really does depend very much on how you use your personality and business acumen. To this extent, Bill has included details about ways to enhance your professional CV by entering into the world of qualified driver training.

This guide will help you decide whether to go ahead with the career or not, and whatever you decide it can help you save a lot of money and time. I would recommend this guide to every single potential driving instructor.

Robin Cummins OBE

Former DSA Chief Driving Examiner

Introduction or preface – A preface is your chance to speak directly to your readers about why you wrote the book, what the book is about, and why it's important. Fiction books do not require a preface. Here are a few useful tips on how to write one:

Within the preface, discuss how the book came about. Tell the readers why you decided to write it, and also why you chose this particular subject. For example, when I wrote the preface to my *How to Become a Firefighter* book I explained how people used to come and ask me for advice on joining the Fire Service, hence the reason I started writing the book. Within the preface, you may also decide to include a brief description of the book. Do not give too much away, but instead give just enough to get the reader interested. Some authors also write about the problems they face when writing or researching the book, and how they overcome those problems. The preface is also a great place to add your acknowledgements. Thank the people who supported you in writing your book, and don't forget to mention any proofreaders, mentors or editors.

Your preface should generally be quite short. The ones I write for my books are usually no more than five pages. You don't want the preface to drag on and on.

At the bottom of your preface/introduction, I recommend you encourage your readers to connect with you on your social media channel(s). I strongly believe every author should have a dedicated Facebook author page from which they can connect with their readers and promote future books and events. To give you an idea of what an author Facebook looks like, head over to mine at **www.facebook.com/richardmcmunnauthor/**

The main chapters of your book

The chapter titles will very much depend on the book genre and main title. For example, chapters for a book on interviews that I would write might be:

CHAPTER 1 – Why do employers use interviews?

CHAPTER 2 – The common mistakes made by people at interviews

CHAPTER 3 – The 10 main reasons why people fail at interviews

CHAPTER 4 – The interview scoring criteria

CHAPTER 5 – How you will be assessed at interviews

CHAPTER 6 – Sample interview questions and answers

CHAPTER 7 – How to easily beat the competition

CHAPTER 8 – 7 ways to impress the interview panel

CHAPTER 9 – Impressing with interview technique

CHAPTER 10 – Useful links and resources

You will notice that the first five chapters are generally negative – I use words such as 'mistakes' and 'fail' – this is deliberate. During the first half of the book I want to 'build the pain'. When it comes to the second half of the book, I want to provide the solution. I use positive words and phrases such as 'easily beat the competition' and 'impress', which leaves the reader feeling upbeat and empowered to achieve.

In fact, a great technique to use when creating chapter titles for your book is to follow these two steps:

STEP 1: Write down the **TRANSFORMATION** your book is going to deliver for your readers, once they have read it. A transformation is basically the outcome or end result the reader will see after they have read and followed the advice contained within your book. For example, the transformation for this book is:

"The reader will be able to write and self-publish a bestselling book."

STEP 2: Once you have your transformation, write down the stepping stones someone will go through to achieve the end goal or result. The stepping stones are effectively your chapter titles! It is your job then, as an author, to add content to each chapter to enable the transformation to be successfully achieved.

Useful links and resources

I have found that most of my readers like me to include a 'useful links and resources' section towards the end of the book. This section will normally include website links and organisations, which the reader will find useful. For example, at the end of this book I have provided a useful links and resources section, that includes details of where to find book cover designers and typesetters etc. This will no doubt be useful information to you.

Disclaimers

I often get asked whether or not an author should include a disclaimer within their book. The answer will very much depend on the type of book that he or she has written. For example, within many of my career-related books, I will provide a simple disclaimer that states that I am not responsible for anyone failing any part of a selection process, as a result of the content within my book. Whilst not essential, this informs the reader that they should only use my information as a guide. It means that I don't have to worry about complex legal repercussions, which commonly arise from giving people advice.

In order to help you, I have provided five sample disclaimers that you may be able to use within your particular book:

Sample book disclaimers

Some names and identifying details have been changed to protect the privacy of individuals. (memoir or recent history)

This is a work of fiction. Names, characters, businesses, places, events and incidents are either the products of the author's imagination or used in a fictitious manner. Any resemblance to actual persons, living or dead, or actual events is purely coincidental. (novels, short stories)

I have tried to recreate events, locales and conversations from my memories of them. In order to maintain their anonymity in some instances I have changed the names of individuals and places, I may have changed some identifying characteristics and details such as physical properties, occupations, and places of residence. (memoir, autobiography)

Although the author and publisher have made every effort to ensure that the information in this book was correct at press time, the author and publisher do not assume and hereby disclaim any liability to any party for any loss, damage, or disruption caused by errors or omissions, whether such errors or omissions result from negligence, accident, or any other cause. (advice, how-to)

This book is not intended as a substitute for the medical advice of physicians. The reader should regularly consult a physician in matters relating to his/her health, and particularly with respect to any symptoms that may require diagnosis or medical attention. (health, alternative healing)

The information in this book is meant to supplement, not replace, proper (name your sport) training. Like any sport involving speed, equipment, balance and environmental factors, (this sport) poses some inherent risk. The authors and publisher advise readers to take full responsibility for their safety and know their limits. Before practicing the skills described in this book, be sure that your equipment is well maintained and do not take risks beyond your level of experience, aptitude, training, and comfort level. (sports, training)

My book writing & publishing action plan

Now, I want to share something very special with you. I am going to provide you with the exact same ACTION PLAN that I have been using for the last few years to consistently publish high-quality books. The action plan that is featured on the following page gives you all the different stages of the process I will follow whenever I sit down to write and publish a book. The plan works for any genre and I encourage you to read it, print it off and stick it in a prominent place at home or in the office where you can refer back to it time and again.

Don't forget, in addition to following the action plan, it is important you set a deadline for which you promise to complete the content for your book. During your writing and publishing journey, make sure you make progress every day, and read the following 7 motivating quotes regularly:

1. If you do nothing, you get nothing. Plan to make progress every day of the week. If you write just one page a day, you are still making progress.

2. Do not be frightened of the writing progress, regardless of your ability levels. Remember where I started, in my cellar, and use that as a motivator to become a bestselling, published author.

3. Swap watching the TV and surfing the Internet for writing content. Stop and think for a minute how many hours you spend each day either watching TV or surfing the Internet. Could you swap this time for writing content? Yes, you could!

4. Write 3 pages a day. After a month, you'll have almost 100 pages of content.

5. Order your book cover design as soon as you have decided on the title and strapline of your book. Once you see the cover design, it will spur you on to finish the content.

6. Consider putting the book on pre-order before you start writing it. If you need a reason to finish the book, this will give you one!

7. Visualise your book on sale through Amazon and on the shelves in high stores such as Waterstones. Visualisation is very powerful!

So, without further ado, here is the action plan for you to follow:

STEP 1 – Generate your book idea

Using the tips supplied in the previous chapter, start to create different ideas for your book. You may find it useful to use my BOOK IDEAS GENERATION

FORM. Once you have come up with your book idea, write it down before moving onto step 2.

$\downarrow$

STEP 2 – Research to see whether or not the book will sell

During step 2 of the action plan, you should use the Google Keyword Planner Tool to ascertain whether or not the book will sell. Type in the anticipated title of your book into the relevant field on the Planner Tool page, using the lessons learnt during the previous chapter.

If you believe that the book will sell, and that there is demand for it, move on to step 3. If there are no people looking for your book idea, consider going back to step 1 or come along to my book writing & publishing training course for help.

$\downarrow$

STEP 3 – Write down the TRANSFORMATION and proposed chapter titles for your book

During step 3, you need to write down the transformation your book is going to deliver and also the proposed chapter titles. The transformation and chapter titles are going to form the structure for your book. If you are writing a fiction book you do not need to create a transformation but you still need to write down the proposed chapter titles/sections for your storyline.

$\downarrow$

STEP 4 – Write the book

During step 4, you need to start writing the content for the book. As a general guide, start writing your manuscript in Microsoft Word, font Arial size 12, with a line spacing of 1.5. Set yourself a target of at least 3 pages every day. If you stick to this you will have written almost 100 pages within a month. Whilst you are writing your book, move onto step 5.

$\downarrow$

STEP 5 – Order the front cover book design artwork

Whilst still writing your book, order the artwork for the front cover. I recommend reading the chapter relating to 'OUTSOURCERS' later on in the book, to learn how to find great book cover designers.

$\downarrow$

STEP 6 – Proofreading and editing

Once you have finished writing the manuscript, and you are 100% happy with the content, send it off to be proofread/edited. Once again, I recommend you refer to the 'OUTSOURCING' chapter to learn how to source professionals in this area. You may also decide at this stage to obtain feedback from a small number of people on your book's content. Be sure to send the content off to people who you know will give you genuine, honest feedback.

$$\downarrow$$

STEP 7 – Typesetting and formatting for Kindle

Once the proofread/edited manuscript is returned to you and you have checked it over to see that you are happy with any changes made, it is now time to get the manuscript typeset for print and formatted for Kindle.

Typesetting is basically the process of preparing the book for print. I recommend that you outsource this element of the book publishing process, as it is important to get it right. I usually send the book cover design to the typesetter, along with the manuscript, so that he or she has an idea of how to brand and style the typesetting to maintain brand consistency. With regards to Kindle formatting, I recommend you refer to a later chapter in the book where I will cover this in more detail.

$$\downarrow$$

STEP 8 – Open your Amazon account to get your book on pre-order.

During step 8 of the action plan, you will need to open your Amazon account. However, before you open your Amazon account, you will need to obtain your ISBN number from Nielsen, as you will need to allocate an ISBN to your book before Amazon will accept it. If you are planning on opening an Amazon KDP account, and you do not wish to try and get your book on sale through Waterstones, then you will not need an ISBN, as Amazon will supply it for you. However, if you do wish to try and get stocked in Waterstones, you will need your own ISBN from Nielsen. Once you have your ISBN, your book can now go on pre-order sale, by following the simple steps in your account.

$$\downarrow$$

STEP 9 – Open your Amazon Kindle Direct Publishing Platform (KDP) account and upload your book

During step 9, you need to get your formatted guide uploaded to Kindle. See a later chapter for more details on how to do this.

STEP 10 – Order your book cover jacket for print

↓

During step 10, you are advised to order the full book cover jacket, which will be required for print. Although you already have the front cover, you will need the jacket, including spine and rear cover, for print purposes. Don't forget to also add the bar code and ISBN to the bottom right hand corner of the rear cover.

↓

STEP 11 – Order your physical books from your chosen printer

Once you receive the typeset guide back from the designer, you must check it over thoroughly, to make sure there are no mistakes. Do not automatically assume the typesetter will not make any mistakes – they can and do creep in at times. Once you are happy with the typeset document, and you have the full book cover jacket, you can now go to print. Whenever I order a new physical book from my printers I will always order a small run of approximately 100-200. See the later section entitled USEFUL LINKS AND RESOURCES for recommended printing companies.

↓

STEP 12 – Launch your physical book on Amazon and send a sample to Gardners books

If you have opted for Amazon KDP, your book will be available to buy as soon as the launch date is reached. Then, as soon as you receive your own books from your chosen printers, you can send off a sample book to Gardners.com, to see if they would be willing to stock it. There will be more about Gardners and getting stocked in Waterstones during a later chapter.

↓

STEP 13 – Market and promote your book

Once your book is published, well done and make sure you celebrate this massive achievement! Not many people get to write and publish a book, so you have done tremendously well to reach STEP 13 of the action plan. During this stage of the process, you will now need to promote your book. Make sure you read the later chapter for some great tips on how to market your book effectively.

The above action plan has always worked for me, and I am sure it will work for you too. It does not matter what genre of book you are writing, give the action plan a try and see how far you get with your book writing and publishing aspirations.

Now let's take a look at the important subject of creating book cover designs and book titles.

CHAPTER 14 –
Book Cover Designs, Book Titles & Straplines

BOOK COVER DESIGNS, BOOK TITLES & STRAPLINES

In this particular chapter, I am going to cover the important subject of book cover designs, book titles and straplines. As you will have probably gathered so far, these three subjects are profoundly important to the success of your writing and publishing strategy. Let's take a look at each one in detail.

Book titles

Your chosen book title can have a huge impact on the number of books that you sell. You will note that my philosophy for choosing book titles is very much focused on what people are searching for online. The Internet is here to stay. As such, you need to focus your strategy on putting your book right under the noses of your customers. If you give people what they are looking for, and you create fantastic content, you will sell lots of books.

Step 1 – Create your book idea

The first step is to use the strategies and tips provided in previous chapters to generate your book idea.

As mentioned previously, a great way to find niche book ideas is to spend time reading the newspapers and online media. Let's assume you have been reading the newspapers one Sunday afternoon, and you notice the following headline:

HOME IS WHERE BUSINESS IS!

The headline clearly indicates that more and more people are starting up a home-based business. The above headline actually featured in a previous copy of THE TIMES, and I saw this as an opportunity for someone to write a book.

Step 2 – Use the Google Keyword Planner to determine search traffic for this subject

Using the methods described previously, I will now go directly to the **Google Planner Keyword Tool** facility, in order to determine what people are searching for online.

I soon realise that there are people searching for information around the very subject **How To Start A Business**:

Ad group ideas	Keyword ideas		
Search Terms		**Avg. monthly searches** [?]	**Competition** [?]
how to start a business	📈	12,100	Medium

There are approximately 12,100 searches for the keyword "How to start a business", a very healthy search phrase from which the basis for a new book could be formed.

The great thing about the **keyword planner tool** is that I am also able to see what the searches are like on a month-by-month basis. In other words, I can determine whether or not there are any seasonal hikes in search traffic. In order to achieve this, simply hover your mouse over the graph as indicated below.

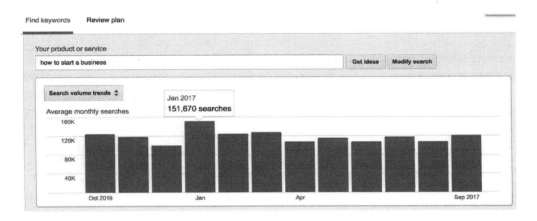

From this graph, I can determine that the searches for this particular search phrase literally are enormous in January (151,670 searches!). This tells me that I will probably sell more of this type of book at the start of the New Year, as people are probably looking for a fresh start. This type of information will also help me to plan ahead with regards to how much physical stock I have available, in order to meet demand for sales on my website.

Step 3 – Go to Amazon.co.uk and see if there is any competition

Once I have determined that there is healthy search traffic for my chosen book subject, I will go to Amazon to see whether there is any competition, and whether it is worth competing in this particular niche.

At the time of writing, there are many books available on starting up business and the ones which have a fantastic book cover design and lengthy/quality content, are selling really well – this tells me there is guaranteed demand for this subject matter/niche and that the book idea is one to press ahead with.

Creating a strapline

Whenever I consider a title for my book, I will almost always add a strapline. A strapline is an extra few words which describe what the book is. Here are a few main book titles, followed by straplines highlighted in grey:

How to become a Firefighter: The ULTIMATE guide to PASSING the Firefighter Selection process

Teacher Interview Questions: Advice and Strategies for PASSING the Teacher Interview

Psychometric Test Questions: 500 Sample Test Questions and Answers

How to Start a Business from Home: Step-by-step advice on starting a home-based BUSINESS

You will notice that I have made use of 'power words' in the first two book title examples – 'ultimate' and 'passing'. You will also notice that I have capitalised these words. I have found that capitalising one or two power words in the strapline helps with conversions. It is certainly worth being creative with your strapline, as this will help your book to stand out from any competitors within your niche.

Another useful way to increase the sales of your book, or sell more than your competitors, is to actually put the current year/version of the book in the strapline. For example, at the time of publication the current year is 2019. For my firefighter book I will call it:

How to become a Firefighter: The ULTIMATE guide to PASSING the Firefighter Selection process, 2019 version

You will notice that by simply adding '2019 version' to the end of my strapline, it automatically makes the book feel fresh and up-to-date. Now, of course, you can only actually add this to your strapline if the book *is* a 2019 version. With most of my books I will update them every year, which qualifies me to add this extra element.

Using numbers in book titles

The use of numbers in book titles, especially for books within genres such as self-help, fitness, motivation, property and business start-up, can be extremely useful in helping with conversions.

Everyone in society is busy. We only have a few spare moments each day to read books and dedicate time to our own self-development. Therefore a book that offers to teach you something within a set time period can be an advantage. Let me give you some examples of book titles, first of all without the number(s) and then with:

BOOK TITLE WITHOUT NUMBERS	BOOK TITLE WITH NUMBERS
How to do press ups	7 weeks to 100 press-ups
How to make money	4 ways to make £1,000 in a week
How to start a business	How to set up a Business in 7 Days from scratch
Yoga for beginners	12 weeks to Yoga success
Job interview questions and answers	147 job interview questions and answers
How to motivate yourself	97 different ways to motivate yourself

You can instantly see how the inclusion of numbers within a book title makes the book more valuable and sellable. The customer can automatically 'feel' the value of the book, as they can see an end result. Including numbers within book titles will also help you to write and construct the book. If you have a specific number to work towards when writing your manuscript, then the book will be far easier to write.

Book cover design

Once we have our book title and strapline, we now need to create the book cover design. It does not matter how good the content is, if the book cover jacket is weak, you will not sell many copies. It's the same analogy when you go to buy a car from a showroom. If the car isn't clean, shiny, polished and immaculately presented, you will not consider buying it. The car is effectively still the same with regards to performance and looks, but because it isn't presented in a way you'd expect it to be, you will not buy it. Make sure you spend plenty of time creating a brilliant book cover design, so as to give your book the best possible chance of selling.

Examples of great book cover designs

I will now show you just a few examples of great book cover designs before going on to tell you how and where to get your own cover created.

ADULT PUZZLE BOOK – HOW2BECOME.COM

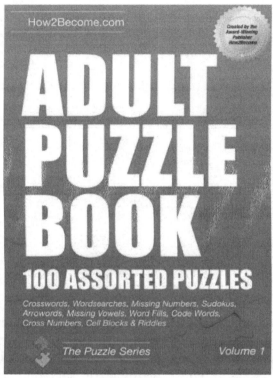

This book cover is clear, simple, niche and provides the perfect description as to what the content is about. When someone online is searching for a book within this niche, they immediately know what the book is about and what it contains. In fact, you don't need me to tell you what the subject is about, simply because the cover design does such a good job of showing you.

HOW TO BECOME A FIREFIGHTER – RICHARD MCMUNN

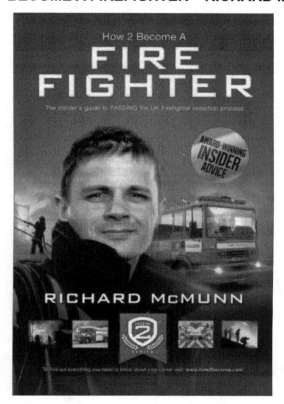

This is the current book cover design for my number-1, bestselling book **how to become a firefighter**. The title and strapline do a great job of telling the reader what the content is about, whilst the image of a firefighter and a fire engine further enhance the visual appeal of the book. Wherever possible, I will also try to match the book cover with the book's subject. This book cover is predominantly red, which is the colour most people will associate with the firefighter job.

THE SPECIAL PARENT'S HANDBOOK – YVONNE NEWBOLD

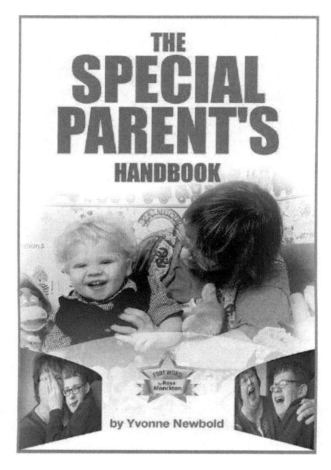

This book was written by Yvonne Newbold, one of the most inspirational women I have ever met. Yvonne joined my **author mentoring programme** a few years ago and worked hard to create fantastic/transformational content. The hard work paid off for Yvonne as her book soon reached number 1 bestseller status on Amazon, not long after launch. Once again, the book cover does a great job of explaining what the content is about.

HOW TO BECOME A DRIVING INTRUCTOR – BILL LAVENDER

This book was written by another author who decided to join my author mentoring programme, Bill Lavender. The book cover design once again does a great job at demonstrating the subject matter and quality/transformational content. This book also achieved number 1 bestseller status and has gone on to sell thousands of copies.

EDUCATING ALICE - J J FITZPATRICK

I worked with JJ Fitzpatrick on my **author mentoring programme** and his bestselling book, Educating Alice, is an example of how an author can use the book's strapline to explain what the content is about. "The Essential 4-Step Guide To Training The Perfect Puppy" does a great job at explaining to the reader what the content is about and how it will benefit the reader.

The above book cover design examples are just a small number of book cover designs that have assisted both my own books, and the books of my author mentoring clients, to become bestsellers.

So, where do I recommend you go to get your book cover design created? There are basically three fantastic outsourcing websites you can use in order to get fantastic book cover designs, as follows:

BookPublishingAcademy.com – This is my own website/service whereby I offer a variety of services, including book cover design, typesetting, Kindle conversion and book printing.

UpWork.com – This is a fantastic outsourcing website you can use to get a variety of tasks outsourced, including book cover design. To find the best book cover designs, go to the following web address:

www.upwork.com/hire/book-cover-design-freelancers/

99Designs.co.uk – This is another great outsourcing website to get your book cover design created.

For further information and advice for hiring book cover designers, please make sure you read and study the dedicated chapter of this book on outsourcing.

GETTING THE FULL BOOK COVER JACKET CREATED

At some point during the book publishing process you will need to get the book cover jacket created in preparation for print. The 'jacket' is the name for the back cover, spine and front cover – all together in one document/PDF. In simple terms, it's what goes on the outside of your book. If you only intend publishing your book through the Kindle platform, then you will only need the front cover design.

To get the full book cover jacket created, you will need the following:

1. The spine width.

2. The text that you want to be included on your spine, including any logo.

3. The rear text for your book, including a photo of you, the author.

4. International Standard Book Number (ISBN).

5. The bar code.

I will now go through each of the above five elements and explain what they are.

The spine width

The way you can ascertain the width of your book spine is to count the number of pages of your typeset book. To give you a rough idea for books that will be digitally printed, I have provided a sample chart below, which includes the number of pages (page extent) and the spine width in millimetres, based on a paper quality of 80GSM.

PAGE EXTENT	80GSM AMBER PREPRINT
64	4.5
72	5
80	5.5
88	6
96	6.5
104	6.5
112	7
120	7.5
128	7.5
136	8
144	8.5
152	9
160	9.5
168	9.5
176	10
184	10.5
192	11
200	11.5
208	11.5
216	12
224	12.5
232	13
240	13.5
248	13.5
256	14
264	14.5
272	15
280	15.5
288	16
296	16.5
304	16.5
312	17

320	17.5
328	18
336	18.5
344	18.5
352	19
360	19.5
368	20
376	20.5

To give you an example, if your book is 112 pages long, then you will need to get your full book cover jacket designed with a 7mm spine. Please note: if your page extent falls between two numbers, always round up to the next spine width thickness. Make sure you contact your chosen book printing company to confirm the exact spine width for your book.

The text that you want to be included on your spine, including any logo

The text that you want to be included on the spine should normally be the TITLE of your book, the author's name, and also a small logo.

The rear text for your book, including a photo of you, the author

There are no rules as to what text you should include on the rear cover; however, to help you decide, the following is an example of what I would normally write:

SAMPLE REAR TEXT FOR YOUR BOOK COVER

How to Become a Driving Instructor is the definitive resource for anyone wishing to obtain a highly sought-after career within the driving industry.

The benefits of working as a driving instructor are many and varied. You can choose your own working hours, and have control over how long your working week is. You will need certain qualities in order to become a driving instructor, such as patience, flexibility, honesty, punctuality, restraint, and diplomacy, amongst others. This guide will teach you how to become a driving instructor, from how to start out, the different training options, lesson plans, and also the different routes available to you in respect of working alone or working through an established driving school.

The guide has been created by driving school professionals, to bring you the very best in expert information and advice.

MAIN PRODUCT FEATURES

- 330 pages of expert information and tutorials.

- How and where to train as a driving instructor.

- The ULTIMATE guide for aspiring driving instructors.

- Written by a leading expert within the driving instructor industry.

About the Author

Bill Lavender is well known for his BETTER TRAINING, featured in the industry magazine *adiNEWS* over the last ten years. He became an Approved Driving Instructor in 1982 and has spent most of his career at the British School of Motoring (BSM) in various senior training and development roles, including NVQ and BTEC awards for instructors. He also was responsible for BSM learning resources, including retail products for learner drivers.

Some authors will also list the different chapters on the rear text, and include a photograph of themselves. Like I say, there are no rules, and it is entirely up to you what you add to the rear cover of your book.

TIP: if you have a website or blog then the rear text is a great place to promote these. Always consider adding your website or blog URL to the rear cover of your book. You should also include a 'call to action' which will serve to encourage the reader to visit your website. An example of this might be:

Visit Richard McMunn's website to get access to your free author toolkit:

www.AuthorToolkit.co.uk

International Standard Book Number (ISBN)

The International Standard Book Number, or ISBN as it is commonly called, is a 13-digit number that uniquely identifies books and book-like products published internationally. The purpose of the ISBN is to establish and identify one title or edition of a title, from one specific publisher. The ISBN is unique to that edition, thus allowing for more efficient marketing of products by booksellers, libraries, universities, wholesalers and distributors.

Every ISBN consists of thirteen digits, and whenever it is printed it is preceded by the letters ISBN. The thirteen-digit number is divided into four parts of variable length, each part separated by a hyphen. The ISBN will usually go just above the barcode, in the bottom right hand corner of the rear cover.

My advice is to purchase your ISBN via the official distributor, Nielsen. Their website, where you can purchase an ISBN and register as a publisher at the same time, is:

www.nielsenisbnstore.com

You will see that the cost for a single ISBN is approximately £89. However, if you purchase 10 x ISBNs, the cost only increases to £159, or thereabouts. My advice is to consider purchasing 10 ISBNs as this will allow you to:

- Write and self-publish further books down the line;

- Use a separate ISBN for the digital versions of your book (Kindle, Kobo, Apple etc.)

There is a piece of software which will create your barcode for you for free. You can download the software from:

http://www.nchsoftware.com/barcode/

The barcode, once generated with your own unique ISBN, will look something like this:

ISBN: 9781909229808

9 781909 229808 >

It is important that the ISBN is also included above the bar code.

Sample full book cover jacket

To give you an idea of how the full jacket cover should look, here is one that we created for one of my own books:

Getting your books printed

Within the publishing industry, you have a couple of printing options, which are listed as follows:

1. Digital (print-on-demand, POD)

2. Litho.

Both have their advantages and disadvantages in terms of cost and quality. Whenever I publish a book, I will usually opt for digital printing, as it enables me to order fewer copies. This enables me to reduce the risk in terms of the initial outlay, whilst I test the market to see how many units the book will sell. If the book is a big seller, I will then order litho copies as these are slightly cheaper, but you do need to order larger runs of this, typically 1,000>.

Printing technology has come a long way in the last 15 years. It's been something of a revolution in the industry, with digital printing starting to replace the more traditional ink based litho printing in many areas. The reason for this is simply because, as a self-publisher, you can produce good quality results in small quantities, at a reasonable cost. Previously the setup costs alone on a litho printing press would have meant that at least 1,000 copies of a book would have to be printed (most printers wouldn't print fewer at that time and still do not), making the entry costs quite high.

Which option is best for a self-published book?

The answer is that it depends on what you are hoping to achieve, and how much you want to risk. There are two basic options:

1. Digital printing (POD), which is great for small numbers of books or if you are only expecting to sell a relatively small number of copies. Digital printing is effectively a very large laser printer, combined with a binding line.

2. Litho printing (ink-based printing), which is better for a larger number of books. This is the traditional form of printing that has been used to produce books for centuries.

My advice is to opt for digital printing initially, until you know how many books you are going to need in the long run.

How much does it cost to get a book printed?

To find out the cost for getting your books printed, please download my book printing pricing calculator at the following website:

www.Book-Printing.net

Now let's move onto the next chapter, which is all about Amazon.

CHAPTER 15 –

Selling Your Books On Amazon

ABOUT AMAZON

Since being founded by Jeff Bezos back in 1995, Amazon has taken the world by storm. It dominates and drives the publishing industry, and has been responsible for bringing us the highly successful Kindle and 'print-on-demand' publishing via Kindle Direct Publishing (KDP) – formally known as CreateSpace.

There are many people and organisations within the publishing industry who detest Amazon, simply because they take such a high profit percentage from authors and publishers alike. My view on Amazon is different. I think they are brilliant and an essential marketplace in which to sell your books to a massive audience. Where else can your book go on sale to a potential 80,000,000 customers every month? If you understand Amazon and how it works, then you can use it to your advantage. In the next two chapters, I will explain how you can do this.

Background to Amazon

In order to understand Amazon and how it can help us to sell thousands of books, we need to first of all understand its history. Amazon was founded in 1995 by Jeff Bezos, and was initially an online book retailer. Books were the very first product that Amazon sold, and it is 'books' which drive the business forward today, despite the fact that they now sell virtually anything and everything!

Amazon was very nearly called **Cadabra**, as in **Abracadabra**. However, because Jeff wanted to sell every product from the alphabet (A to Z), the name he settled on was **Amazon.** Amazon is the longest river in the world, it starts with the letter 'A' and it also represents significant 'volume' and 'depth'.

Over recent years, a large number of high street booksellers have either gone into administration, or if they haven't, they have seen their profits drop significantly. The reason for this is twofold:

1. Consumers are choosing to buy their books and general goods online – this trend will continue;

2. Amazon offers consumers excellent customer service and fast delivery, at low prices.

High street bookstores simply cannot compete with Amazon, for the following reasons:

1. A standard brick and mortar high street book store can hold approximately 200,000 physical books, whereas Amazon can stock unlimited numbers of books;

2. With more and more consumers switching to the Internet in order to buy their books and other goods, high street book stores will suffer and will continue to do so;

3. Because Amazon is not a 'face-to-face' retailer, it is able to keep its costs down;

4. Due to the unbelievably large number of transactions that Amazon takes every day, it is able to negotiate excellent postal rates with the likes of Royal Mail and other mail/package delivery companies. This effectively enables Amazon to offer FREE postage and package to its customers;

5. High street bookstores are not very good at 'capturing' customer's details when they walk through their shop front door. This is a shame, because it is these details which could be used for future marketing promotions. Once you buy one product from Amazon, they will then email you every week to offer you extra goods and products – this is called the 'upsell'.

Amazon customer service

The Amazon logo represents a large 'smile', which indicates how obsessed they are with providing great customer service. If you complain to Amazon as a customer, they will either sort it out for you ASAP or refund your payment. Their exceptional level of customer service is another reason why Amazon has done so well. Ask yourself the following question – how many times have you received poor customer service from a high street shop? I have experienced it many times in the past, yet I have never received poor customer service from Amazon.

Now ask yourself another question – how many times have you gone to buy products from a high street store, only to find that they don't have your size or what you want in stock? Again, this has happened to me many times, and all it does is force me to shop online with retailers such as Amazon, where I *know* they will have what I want and will be able to deliver within 24 hours.

The great thing about selling your books on Amazon is that this outstanding level of customer service is all set up to help you. You do not have to employ any staff. You do not have to send your books to your customers, and you also do not have to deal with any customer service enquiries or complaints – Amazon will do all of this for you.

The Amazon loss leader

For those people who understand sales and marketing, you will undoubtedly be familiar with the term 'loss leader'. A loss leader can be described as:

"A product sold at a low price (at cost or below cost) in order to stimulate other profitable sales."

Amazon is the master of the loss leader. It uses 'books' as a way to draw customers into their database. Then, once a person has made their first purchase, Amazon will try to sell them additional goods both immediately on their sales-page and also by way of email promotions after the initial purchase.

If you have previously purchased something from Amazon, start to take note of how often they email you with follow-up offers and promotions – they are extremely clever at what they do, and as an author/self-publisher you are going to take advantage of their outstanding marketing systems.

HOW TO SELL YOUR BOOKS ON AMAZON

During the next few pages I am going to teach you how to sell your book(s) on Amazon. Now that we know a little about Amazon's history and how it works we can start to put the pieces of the selling process together. To begin with, let's take a look at the Amazon sales-page.

The Amazon sales-page explained

When you next go to the Amazon website, take a look at any page on their site that is selling a book. On each sales page there are a number of **POINTS OF INTEREST,** which I believe you need to fully understand when self-publishing books:

POINT OF INTEREST 1: The book title and strapline

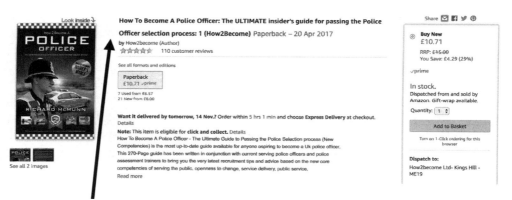

The title and strapline of your book can be found here.

The title and strapline of your book have a significant impact on how your book will be listed on Amazon, and also in search engines such as Google and Bing.

As we established earlier, we need to name our book with a phrase that is relevant to what people are searching for, both on the search engines and also on Amazon.

For example, if I wanted to write and publish a book that teaches people **how to write a business plan** for a new business, I would call it one of the following:

- How To Write A Business Plan!

- How To Write A Business Plan: An ESSENTIAL guide for NEW Business Start-Ups!

- How To Write A Business Plan: The ULTIMATE guide for writing Business Plans!

- How To Write A Business Plan for Beginners.

You will notice that I have used the main focus of the book (how to write a business plan) at the start of the overall title. This is for the following reasons:

1. This title is easy to understand, and it tells the customer EXACTLY what the book is about and what it will do for them;

2. I want the search engines and Amazon to list this book on the first page for the phrase 'how to write a business plan'. If the book title is 'relevant' to what people are searching for, it will have a better chance of ranking in the search pages on Google and Amazon.

To give you an example of how I have used this method to great success over the years, here is a sample case study:

Recently, I worked closely with an author called Bill Lavender through my **one-to-one author mentoring programme**, to help him publish a book that teaches people how to become a driving instructor. Bill is a highly-experienced driving instructor, and he wanted to publish a book that would help people achieve their goal. I initially carried out some research using the Google Keyword Planner tool, and established that 6,600 people were searching for the phrase 'how to become a driving instructor'.

I then turned my attentions to Amazon, and found that no other author or publisher was selling a book using the exact same title. There were, however, a small number of people selling books on the same subject, albeit with different titles such as:

- **The Driving Instructor's Handbook**

- **Become an Approved Driving Instructor**

- **How to land a top-paying Driving Instructor's job**

Now, I am not saying that these titles are poor, because they are not. I am also not saying that the books will not sell, far from it. What I am saying is that my strategy and approach for naming books, to exactly what people are searching for, makes perfect sense. Furthermore, it works. If you create a product or service and then put it right under the noses of the customers who are searching for it, you will have a better chance of making a sale. If you go to Amazon.co.uk right now and type in 'how to become a driving instructor' you will see Bill's book right at the top of the listings for that search term.

It is important to point out at this stage that just because you use a title/name that your customers are searching for, it will not automatically equal a rank at number 1 spot for that search term. There are other important factors that have an influence, too, such as the reviews, the number of sales, and also the number of books that your book is **frequently bought together** with.

POINT OF INTEREST 2: The front cover design of the book

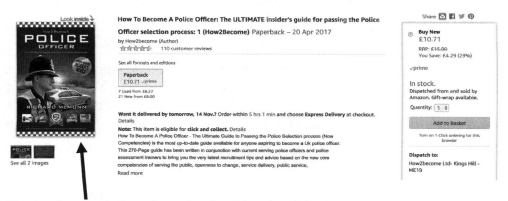

The front cover design of your book will be shown here.

When selling on Amazon, and online in general, you should always aim for simplicity and quality. When a person visits a website or sales-page, you literally have just a few seconds to gain their interest in your product or service. If you do not gain their interest they will go elsewhere. To prove this point, I encourage you to think carefully about how you personally search for goods and services online, and how long you stay on a particular website whilst surfing. When you next search the web for a particular product or service, think about those websites that make you stay and ask yourself the question — 'What makes me stay on this website?' It might be the quality of the website you are visiting, the level of trust it offers, or more likely it will be the fact that they offer exactly what you are looking for.

With regards to your book cover, try to think about your customers and what they would want. Too many authors and publishers create book covers that have little relevance to the book title or subject. Your job is to make the customer click the BUY NOW button, and creating quality and relevant book covers will certainly help with the conversion rate.

POINT OF INTEREST 3: The book's description

Your book's description will be shown here.

The book description is your opportunity to 'sell' your book to the customer. Most customers will read the description before deciding whether or not to click the BUY NOW button. Therefore, it is important that it is free from mistakes, grammatically correct, and uses positive words to describe how the book will be of benefit to the reader. Here are some great tips that will help you to construct a great book description:

TIP 1. When writing the book description, the only thing that matters is the main plot or main theme of the book. Do not overcomplicate the description, and always consider the fact that the customer will want to make a relatively fast decision on whether or not to buy your book.

TIP 2. Keep it under 200 words. There are no rules with regards to how long or short your description should be, but I have tested both very short descriptions and also ones that are in excess of 500 words. In summary, I have found that those that are between 150 and 200 words convert better. In the simplest terms, when writing your book description, concentrate on what your book is about and what your readers will find interesting about it. You may also find it useful to include the chapter titles within your description.

TIP 3. Write in third person, present tense. When describing your book, think as if you are sitting face-to-face with the reader. Pretend they have asked you what the book is about.

TIP 4. Repeat the title of the book 2-3 times in the description, but no more. When writing my book descriptions, I will always start off with the title of the book. I will then include it one or two times more throughout the duration of the description. The reason that I do this is solely for search engine optimisation purposes, as I want the books sales-page to rank on the major search engines for the title of the book.

TIP 5. Use emotional 'power words' in the description. My advice would be to use approximately 5-10 power words within your book's description. Power words are used to evoke emotion, and they will certainly help to increase conversions. Just make sure the power words are relevant to the content of your book, and also relevant to your books genre.

Examples of power words for novels and fiction books include:

Amazing, Audacity, Backbone, Belief, Blissful, Bravery, Breathtaking, Cheer, Conquer, Courage, Daring, Defiance, Delight, Devoted, Excited, Eye-opening, Faith, Fearless, Fulfil, Grateful, Grit, Guts, Happy, Heart, Hero, Hope, Jaw-dropping, Jubilant, Magic, Mind-blowing, Miracle, Pluck, Sensational, Spectacular, Spirit, Stunning, Surprising, Triumph, Uplifting, Valour, Victory, Wonderful and Wondrous.

Examples of power words for self-help, motivational and business start-up books include:

Accomplished, Attentive, Benevolent, Bold, Bright, Brilliant, Captivating, Caring, Compassionate, Conscious, Constant, Courageous, Courteous, Dedicated, Determined, Disciplined, Effective, Energetic, Engaging, Entertaining, Enthusiastic, Equitable, Expressive, Exquisite, Extraordinary, Fascinating, Fearless, Flexible, Fortunate, Friendly, Generous, Genuine, Glorious, Gracious, Gutsy, Helpful, Honourable, Immense, Incredible, Ingenious, Inspiring, Intelligent, Intuitive, Inventive, Majestic, Marvellous, Motivating, Optimistic, Original, Passionate, Perceptive, Persistent, Pleasing, Powerful, Quick-minded, Remarkable, Resourceful, Rousing, Sensational, Sincere, Stunning, Understanding, Unique and Venturous.

TIP 6. Write the description as if you are the publisher, not the author. Making an impact on the reader is your principal concern. Your job is to make sure the reader finishes reading the description, with a desire to want to find out more. Remember, the book description is marketing material – not literature.

POINT OF INTEREST 4: Book reviews and Amazon Verified Purchases

Top customer reviews

Chris

⭐⭐⭐⭐⭐ **A Big help!**

8 September 2017

Format: Paperback | **Verified Purchase**

Great book, complete run through of every stage of the selection process with loads of hints and tips

Comment | One person found this helpful. Was this review helpful to you? | Yes | No | Report abuse

Amazon Verified Purchases can help your book rankings.

Book reviews have a massive impact on your sales. I have known a number of authors who spent months or sometimes years writing their book, only for it to receive 1 or 2 star reviews once it is published, and the book sales plummet as a consequence.

There is no golden formula for getting positive reviews for your book, apart from writing and publishing a book that deserves them. My advice is to simply concentrate on writing and publishing a HIGH QUALITY book – if you do this, the positive reviews will follow naturally.

There are a number of different ways in which you can obtain fake or engineered reviews, but my advice is to steer well clear of these. The main problem with this, apart from the fact that it is against Amazon's terms and conditions, is that your readers can see right through a fake or engineered review, and they may leave a comment on the review questioning its validity. Readers of your reviews also have the opportunity to 'VOTE' up or down the reviews your book receives, so if the readers of your review(s) find one of them to be particularly helpful, regardless of the fact of whether it's 1 star or 5 star, that review will go up to the top of the review rankings for your book. If it's a 1 star review that they find the most helpful, sales of your book will literally dry up!

A few years back, Amazon introduced something that is called the **AMAZON VERIFIED PURCHASE (AVP).** This was in direct response to many authors, publishers and general sellers of goods on Amazon complaining that too many people were leaving fake or engineered reviews on their products in an attempt to boost their sales and rakings.

When a product review is marked "Amazon Verified Purchase", it means that the customer who wrote the review actually purchased the item directly from Amazon. Customers can add this label to their review, provided that Amazon can verify that the item being reviewed was purchased on Amazon. co.uk. Customers reading an **Amazon Verified Purchase** review can use this information to help them to decide which reviews are most helpful in their purchasing decisions.

If a review is not marked Amazon Verified Purchase, it doesn't mean that the reviewer has no experience with the product – it just means that Amazon couldn't verify that it had been purchased from Amazon. The customer may have purchased the item elsewhere or had another interaction with it. The Amazon Verified Purchase Review label offers one more way to help gauge the quality and relevance of a product review.

The whole point of me raising the AVP system on Amazon is to simply state the obvious – the more positive Amazon Verified Purchase reviews your book obtains on Amazon, the more likely it will sell better.

TIP: There is absolutely nothing wrong with you asking people within your network to buy your book direct from Amazon and then leave a review. It is important, however, to ask those people to provide a review that is both honest and genuine and based on their actual experiences of the book and how it helped them. You MUST NOT try to influence them in anyway. If they leave a poor review then you must use their comments to improve the book for the next print-run or revised edition.

Reasons why people leave poor reviews

Here are a number of reasons why people leave poor reviews on books, and how you can avoid them:

1. **Poor formatting on the Kindle versions.** When getting your book formatted for Kindle, be sure to use a reputable company, or someone who at least knows what they are doing. The danger with trying to format your book yourself is that you are more likely to make a mistake, and the book will not read properly on the Kindle reading device. If there are errors with the formatting, people will probably leave a poor review. Read the chapter on outsourcing, to learn how to hire professionals who can format your Kindle book.

2. **Poor customer service or delivery issues.** The good thing about this is that people who buy your book direct from Amazon will probably experience great customer service and fast delivery. If they buy your book direct from your own website or blog, and the delivery is slow or customer service sub-standard, they may well head to Amazon to leave you a negative review. If selling a book from your own website, be sure to provide excellent customer service.

3. **Mistakes, poor grammar, spelling and punctuation.** If your book is riddled with errors then people will almost always leave a negative review. Of course, it is very difficult to write and publish a book that is totally error-free, and if there are just one or two slight issues with the content then most readers will forgive this. However, if it is clear to the reader that the author has made little or no effort to get the book checked, proofread or edited, then a negative review is likely.

To summarise, the only real way to gain fantastic reviews of your book is to write and publish great content that your readers will love.

POINT OF INTEREST 5: Your book's ranking (getting to bestseller!)

Product details

Paperback: 130 pages

Publisher: How2Become Ltd (18 Aug. 2017)

Language: English

ISBN-10: 1911259881

ISBN-13: 978-1911259886

Product Dimensions: 17 x 0.8 x 24.5 cm

Average Customer Review: ⭐⭐⭐⭐⭐ ▾ 3 customer reviews

Amazon Bestsellers Rank: 4,971 in Books (See Top 100 in Books)
  #55 in Books > Sports, Hobbies & Games > Hobbies & Games > **Puzzles & Quizzes**

Would you like to **tell us about a lower price**?
If you are a seller for this product, would you like to **suggest updates through seller support**?

Get in the top 100 for any category on Amazon and your book is a bestseller!

Your book's ranking will not generally have any impact on conversion rate, simply because your average customer will not be aware that the Amazon book rankings exist. To you, however, a book's ranking is very important. If your book manages to rank in the top 100 of any category on Amazon, you are automatically a bestseller, and this 'status' can be used to help promote your book.

Amazon's book rankings are not that easy to understand, and there do not seem to be many people who understand them outside of Amazon. However, from my own experience of selling on Amazon for a number of years, here's what I *do* know:

-   Amazon's book rankings are updated every hour.

-   If a customer purchases a book on Amazon, it may not get registered as a sale on the book ranking system for a few hours.

-   Amazon lists approximately 8 million books.

-   If a book does not have any ranking, this means it hasn't sold any copies.

-    If you see a book with a rank in the four or five million range, you'll know it's a poor seller.

-    A book's rank will change hourly, unless it has not sold any copies. A book may gain a good rank due to a burst of sales, but if it doesn't sell anymore after that then it will gradually fall down the rankings.

-    Each book is ranked against every other book sold on Amazon. To put it simply, the smaller the number your book's rank is, the better, and if you have a ranking of 4,000, it means that 3,999 books are ahead of you in terms of book sales.

-    In general, a ranking in the five digits, say 30,000, means that your book is selling relatively well on Amazon. Many of my books consistently rank in the top 10,000 on Amazon, every hour of the day. Be aware though that selling just one copy can temporarily skyrocket you up the rankings (on an hourly basis), so don't assume that a five-digit ranking means you've sold a large quantity of books. Either way, you'll be able to check your sales figures via your KDP account.

The following is not exact; however it will give you a rough indication as to how many books you might sell based on a particular ranking:

Amazon Bestseller-Rank	Estimated book sales per week
10,000	30
100,000	6
1,000,000	< 1

Disclaimer: The Amazon book ranking changes continuously, and therefore the information provided here is not guaranteed – it is simply a guide.

POINT OF INTEREST 6: Frequently bought together

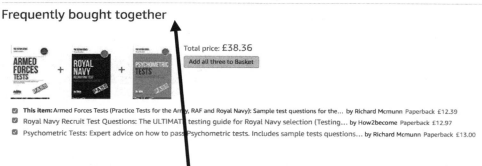

Your book will sell better if listed with other books in the FREQUENTLY BOUGHT TOGETHER area of the Amazon sales-page.

Amazon is the master of the upsell! At every opportunity, Amazon is trying to tempt you into buying additional items – this is great news for you as an author and self-publisher.

On the Amazon sales-page you will see the **FREQUENTLY BOUGHT TOGETHER** (FBT) options. These are books that have often been purchased in conjunction with the main item being listed on that particular page. You will notice that the FBT options are presented along with a BUY NOW button, which says something like 'Add all three to basket'. The customer will also have the option to remove one or more of the additional FBT items listed, based on their preferences. The aim of the game is to get your book listed with as many other books as possible in the FBT area of the sales-page. If you manage to achieve this, sales will increase significantly. If you can manage to get your book listed on the FBT section with another bestseller you are onto a winner!

POINT OF INTEREST 7: Customers Who Bought This Item Also Bought

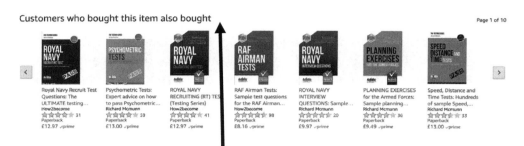

Customers who bought this item also bought   Page 1 of 10

The more your book sells with other books, the further to the left it will appear on the 'Customers Who Bought This Also Bought' section.

This area of the Amazon sales-page works in conjunction with the FREQUENTLY BOUGHT TOGETHER section. If one person buys your book along with another, you will automatically get listed in this section. The more times your book is purchased with a particular book, the further to the left of the page your book will move. Eventually it will make its way up to the FREQUENTLY BOUGHT TOGETHER section. The problem is with some books is that there are many pages of 'Customers Who Bought This Also Bought', and therefore it could take some time before your book makes it along the pages, and finally ends up in the page 1 FREQUENTLY BOUGHT TOGETHER area for a particular book.

If you are like me, and intend on writing and publishing a series of books, then the aim is to get all your books on the first page of the 'Customers Who Bought This Also Bought', and into the FBT section. You will see from my ARMED FORCES TESTS book sales-page on Amazon, that every book featured on the 'Customers Who Bought This Also Bought' section and the FBT section belongs to me.

POINT OF INTEREST 8: Your Amazon author page

The majority of authors selling their books on Amazon do not take the time to create an 'author page'. To create a proper author page, you will need to sign up at the following link:

https://authorcentral.amazon.co.uk

Alternatively, simply search for 'Amazon Author Central' in Google and you will see the relevant page appear.

It is very important that you set up your Amazon Author page for the following reasons:

1. A dedicated author page will help you to build trust with your customers and readers.

2. If a customer can see the 'real' person behind the book, they are more likely to click the BUY NOW button.

3. When you set up your author page, you will be able to add a photograph, a biography, and a video. Make sure you add a video to your author page as it can have a positive effect on your book sales!

4. When you access your dedicated author's page, you will be able to review your sales ranking statistics for all of your books (updated hourly). In addition to this, you will also be able to see any customer reviews and what people are saying about your books. This is particularly useful if you have lots of books on sale with Amazon. If you receive any negative reviews of your book(s) on Amazon, then you may want to take the opportunity to inform the reviewer that you will take their feedback on board, and review the book for the next edition.

Tips for creating your author biography

1. Keep it relatively short. Between 150 and 200 words will be sufficient.

2. Write your biography as if you are speaking to the person reading it.

3. Try including the following in your biography:

   - Who you are;

   - Your experiences, qualifications and background;

   - Why you decided to write your book(s);

   - The aim of your book(s);

   - How your book(s) will be of benefit to the reader.

Now that we have covered the key elements of the Amazon sales page, let's now move onto the account I recommend you use in order to get your book published on Amazon.

AMAZON KINDLE DIRECT PUBLISHING PROGRAMME (FORMALLY CREATESPACE)

Kindle Direct Publishing (KDP) is a fantastic place to get your book self-published. Not only will Amazon deal with all the customer service side of things, including handling customer queries and posting the books out to your customers, but they will also print the book for you once an order is placed. This means you do not have to send any stock off to Amazon! Perfect if you are a self-publishing author who is doing this in your spare time.

Overview of KDP

Amazon KDP offers free tools and professional services to help make the entire publishing and distribution process cost-effective, fast, and easy-to-use. Printing, manufacturing and shipping is taken care of, so you do not have to order your own books from a 3rd party printer. Your book will remain in stock and never run out.

Some of the benefits to publishing on KDP

- Book covers are printed in full-colour and laminated for durability;

- Professional quality trade paperback binding;

- Printed on white or cream paper;

- Free ISBN will be supplied, if you do not already have one.

KDP royalties and the payment system

The royalty system with KDP will depend on a number of factors, including:

- The trim size of your book (you can choose this yourself);

- The number of pages of your book;

- Interior type (black & white, full colour etc.)

To give you an example, a 200-page book, printed in black & white with a trim size of 5" x 8" (industry standard), and with a retail price of £13, will give you a royalty of approximately £5.10 per unit sold. This is certainly comparable with royalties that I personally receive from a similar size and style of book through the Advantage programme. Although the royalty standards are different for each programme, I personally get excellent rates with my UK-based printer (per unit) which allows me to make more per book sale than your average book publisher.

You can sign up for a KDP programme here:

kdp.amazon.com

It is extremely simple to upload your book to Amazon KDP. However, if you get stuck, and you need a bit of help, watch the video that is contained within the free Author Toolkit at the following website:

www.AuthorToolkit.co.uk

CHAPTER 16 –
Kindle and Ebooks

KINDLE AND EBOOKS

Electronic book publishing, particularly on Amazon Kindle, has taken the publishing world by storm. Whilst many UK-based publishers rue the fact that Amazon dominates this rapidly expanding market, many writers and authors across the world are seeing handsome returns for their writing efforts. The fact that writers like you are now getting rewarded appropriately for their writing skills is, in my opinion, long overdue.

For too long writers received very low royalty rates for their work. However, the introduction of the Amazon Kindle back in 2007 levelled the playing field, which meant one thing for authors across the world – more profits and greater exposure for their book.

Publishing on the **Amazon Kindle Direct Publishing Platform** is a fast and efficient way to get your book in front of literally millions of readers worldwide. Here are just a few benefits of publishing your book on the Kindle:

✓ No face-to-face selling or having to deal with customer service/fulfilment;

✓ Amazon will electronically deliver the eBook for you;

✓ There are NO customer emails to deal with;

✓ Amazon has millions of customers worldwide (approximately 80,000,000 per month). Publish your book once and it will reach a global market;

✓ There are no set-up fees to start selling your book on the Kindle;

✓ The Amazon Kindle Direct Publishing Platform has a fast set-up process. Publishing takes less than 5 minutes. Your book appears on Amazon within 24 hours;

✓ Amazon is a '24/7 – 365 days a year' operation which means your book sells whilst you sleep;

✓ You get very good support from Amazon;

✓ You still have the option to upsell within a Kindle book;

✓ You get to keep control, and you can make changes to your book at any time;

✓ You can earn a 70% royalty on every book you sell;

✓ You can publish in multiple languages, including English, German, French, Spanish, Portuguese, Italian, and Japanese.

Kindle Direct Publishing Select (KDP Select)

Amazon has also introduced what is called the KDP Select Global Fund. A share of this fund is available to authors and publishers who allow other people to read their book for free. At the date of this book's publication, the Global Fund was a staggering $19.5 Million.

What is the Kindle Owners' Lending Library?

The Kindle Owners' Lending Library is a collection of books that Amazon Prime members who own a Kindle can borrow once a month, for no fee. Your books will still be available for anyone to buy in the Kindle Store, and you'll continue to earn royalties from those sales like you normally would.

What does it mean to publish exclusively on Kindle?

When you choose to enrol your book in KDP Select, you're committing to make the digital format of that book available exclusively through KDP. During the period of exclusivity, you cannot distribute your book digitally anywhere else, including on your website, blogs, etc. However, you can continue to distribute your book in physical format, or in any format other than digital.

From a personal perspective, I have found that KDP select is worth enrolling in, as my royalties have increased for Kindle books that are part of the programme – the only real issue for you is that you won't be able to sell the Kindle book anywhere else, not even on your own website.

TIP: You can still promote your book on your website, but you will need to link through to the Amazon sales page.

HOW TO GET YOUR BOOK READY TO SELL ON KINDLE

To sell your book on the Amazon Kindle Direct Publishing Platform, you will need:

1. Your manuscript converted to a suitable format for Kindle.

2. The front cover of your book in JPEG format. JPEG, or JPG, is a common term used for a common file format for digital photos and other digital graphics.

3. An Amazon Kindle KDP account.

Let's take a look at each area individually.

Converting your manuscript for Kindle

There are many companies and individuals online who will offer to format your book for Kindle, and my advice is to use one of them, providing they are professional and good at what they do.

Most people try to convert their book themselves using free online Kindle conversion software tools or by following Amazon's advice and free step-by-step guide on how to do it yourself. Whilst these tools do work, they will usually always leave formatting errors within the book. My advice is to employ the services of an outsourcer to format your book for you.

The great thing about Kindle, from a customer/reader's perspective, is that Amazon offers a 7-day money back guarantee on Kindle eBooks. Here's what Amazon says on their website about refunds:

"Books that you purchase from the Kindle Store are eligible for return and refund, if we receive your request within 7 days of the date of purchase. Once a refund is issued, you will no longer have access to the book."

One of the most important aspects of publishing on Kindle is to give no reason for your customers to request a refund. Regardless of how good your content is, if you mess up with the formatting, customers WILL request a refund. What's even worse, they will most probably then also leave a negative review on your book – and we all know what impact a negative review can have!

My advice would be to get the book formatted by a professional individual or organisation. Personally, I use Upwork.com to get my books converted, and I usually pay approximately $70-$100 for a book which contains approximately 150-200 pages. The cost for conversion when using Upwork.com will very much depend on the complexity of the book. For example, if there are lots of images or charts within the content then this will increase the price. Before you go ahead and hire a professional outsourcer to format your book, please make sure that you read the relevant chapter on outsourcing, as it will help you to avoid the common pitfalls.

You will need to send the outsourcer both your completed manuscript (preferably in Word) and the front book cover image in JPEG format. For Kindle conversion, you do not need to get the full book cover jacket created with spine and rear text. You also do not need to add the ISBN or bar code to the cover; just the front book cover will be fine.

Compatible format types accepted by Amazon

Kindle Direct Publishing (KDP) lets you upload and convert your final draft from several formats. For best results, Amazon recommends that you upload in DOC/DOCX (.doc/.docx) or HTML (.html) format. However, from personal experience I have always formatted my book in ePub. The reason for this is that the Apple iBookStore and Gardners eWarehouse will only accept eBooks in ePub format. Therefore, in order to save on cost, it is advisable to get your book formatted in ePub, and you can then sell it through multiple channels.

Here is the full list of formats accepted by Amazon DTP:

- Word (DOC or DOCX)

- HTML (ZIP, HTM, or HTML)

- MOBI (MOBI)

- ePub (EPUB)

- Rich Text Format (RTF)

- Plain Text (TXT)

- Adobe PDF (PDF)

Using the Amazon Kindle Book Cover Creator

Amazon provides a free book cover creator. I have used it on a number of occasions, and whilst the quality is not as good as using a professional designer, it is a good way to get started if your budget is low. Having said that, remember the advice I have provided in previous sections regarding the importance of book cover design – if you get it wrong, you won't sell many copies!

In order to use the Kindle Cover Creator, click on the "Add new title" button once you are signed into your account. Next, click "Design with Cover Creator" in section 4, then "Upload Your Cover." The Cover Creator interface will automatically launch, and instructions will then be provided on how to create your cover.

As I have already mentioned on numerous occasions, the image you use for your cover will be the first thing that people see when they find your book, so choose an image that really represents the quality and subject of your work. You can provide your own image or select from the gallery of stock images available.

Images you provide should be of high quality, and you must hold all rights necessary to use the image for your book cover.

Choosing a Design

After you've uploaded or selected your image, you can choose from one of ten base designs, which can then be further customized with various layouts as well as font and colour schemes. In case you can't find an image you're satisfied with, Amazon has included some basic designs that don't incorporate an image from your computer or the stock image gallery.

Customising your layout

Once you've selected a base design, you can choose from an assortment of font sets, colour schemes, and text layouts or make changes to your text and images directly by clicking on each part.

Previewing and submitting your cover

When you have completed designing your cover, click the "Preview Cover" button to check how it looks in colour, grayscale, and thumbnail modes.

Once you're satisfied with your cover, click "Save & Submit" to submit your cover to KDP. Cover Creator will close and your cover will be loaded in the "Edit book details" page of KDP.

Using An External Cover

If you've had the cover made elsewhere (something I recommend you do), then you'll need to turn the main/front cover image from the full jacket into a thumbnail. This is very simple to do, as I'll outline below:

- Once you arrive on the KDP page, you'll see an option to 'submit your own cover'. Click this.

- Next, open up your full jacket or the front cover on its own. I would highly recommend using GIMP software for this. This is completely free, and you can download it online.

- Once you arrive in GIMP or your photo editing software, all you need to do is crop the image, so that only the front cover is left.

- Following this, you'll need to resize the image. Images uploaded to Kindle as a thumbnail need to be at least 1000 pixels in height. You can change this in GIMP by clicking 'image' (at the top), then scale image, then change the height to 1000. Make sure the tiny lock to the right is locked, and not open. Now click inside the width box. If you've done this right, the width should change all by itself, corresponding with the changed height.

- The last step is exporting the image. Instead of just saving it, click 'file' and then 'export as'. Manually change the type of file to .jpeg (you can do this by just editing the end of the name in the save bar), and then click export. Finally, change the quality to 100 on the scroll bar that appears, and you're done! All you need to do now is select the new file when it comes to uploading the thumbnail.

Getting paid by Amazon for Kindle sales

Separate royalty payments for each Kindle Store will be paid automatically by Electronic Funds Transfer (EFT), Wire Transfer (where available), or cheque approximately sixty (60) days following the end of the calendar month. Keep in mind that your bank may charge fees for some payments. If you're not sure whether they do, you may want to contact them.

How to see how many Kindle books you have sold

In your Amazon KDP account there are a number of reports available for you to view at any time, and these are listed as follows:

Month-to-Date Unit Sales

You can use this report to get a quick snapshot of your unit sales and transactions for the current month's sales.

Prior Six Weeks' Royalties

This report shows transactions and royalties that you've earned over the six weeks prior to the current week.

Prior Months' Royalties

These reports show summaries of previous months' sales transactions, for the last 12 months. Reports are generated near the 15th day of each month and include sales that occurred within the prior month.

HOW TO UPLOAD YOUR BOOK TO THE AMAZON KINDLE DIRECT PUBLISHING PLATFORM, PLUS USEFUL TIPS

In this section of the chapter, I will show you how to upload a book to your Amazon Kindle Direct Publishing Platform.

STEP 1 – Open your account

In order to open your account, please go to:

https://kdp.amazon.com/

STEP 2 – Add new title

Once you have signed up for your account, completed the tax information and logged in, please now click the **CREATE NEW TITLE > +Kindle ebook button** which is located in the top left hand corner of the dashboard.

STEP 3 – Consider choosing Kindle Select

One of the first decisions that you will need to make when it comes to uploading your eBook is whether or not to enrol your book in Kindle select.

If you decide to include your eBook in Kindle Select, you are enrolling for 90 days, during which time your eBook must not be available in digital format on any other platform. If your book is found to be available elsewhere in digital format, it may not be eligible to remain in the program.

The decision on whether to include your book in KDP Select is entirely yours. As previously mentioned, the programme has been beneficial for me.

STEP 4 – Enter your book's details

In the next section of your account area, you will need to add the details of your book.

- *Book name*

Taking what you have learnt so far, input the name of your book in this field. You just need to input the main title of your book, and not the subtitle or strapline.

- *Subtitle (optional)*

The subtitle is your book's strapline. Although it says 'optional' my advice would be to insert one, especially if your genre falls into anything outside of fiction. A subtitle will be picked up in the search engines, which may help with conversions.

- *This book part of a series*

If your book is part of a series, insert it here. For example, my books fall under the 'How2Become' series. Once your brand becomes established and readers learn to love your books, they will start to search for your brand or series of books. If you intend on publishing more than one book, consider having a series name.

- *Edition number (optional)*

Providing the version number can help readers to know whether the book is the original edition, or if it contains updated content. If this is the first time you have published this book, enter the numeral 1. If the book was previously published and the version you are publishing contains significant changes, enter the numeral 2 (and so on).

- *Publisher (optional)*

Because you will be the author and publisher of your book, you can enter your name or the name of your publishing company here.

- *Description*

Your book description is what customers see as they shop in the Kindle store. If you are publishing a printed version too, the description should be the same. Within the description, I recommend that you consider including the main title of the book 2-3 times. This will help your book to rank in the search results.

- *Book contributors*

Contributors are the people who have helped you to create your book. Within this field you can add and identify your book's author, editor, illustrator, translator, and more. If the book has more than one author, you can enter multiple authors. Enter author names in the sequence that you would like them to appear in the Kindle store. To publish your book, at least one contributor name is required. The first person you should add as a contributor is yourself as the 'author'.

- *Language*

In this field, input the primary language in which the book has been written.

- *Publication date (optional)*

This is the date that you are publishing the book. Simply leave it blank or select the date that you are publishing your eBook. Alternatively, if you already have the same book published in print-format, select the date that the physical version was published.

TIP: Selecting a publication date will inform customers of how up-to-date your book is – this will help with conversion.

- ISBN (optional)

As previously stated, the ISBN is an International Standard Book Number. You do not need to have an ISBN to publish your Kindle book, but if you do have one, then enter it in this section. You can purchase an ISBN from the official ISBN body, Nielsen at the following website:

www.nielsenisbnstore.com

- Verify your publishing rights

'Publishing rights' are the rights that you need to have in order to publish a book. To publish a book for Kindle through KDP, you must have obtained all rights necessary to publish the digital book from the book's author and any other content creators. If you are the book's author, you must have retained all of the necessary digital book publishing rights. If you are both the author and publisher, as is the case for most of my books, you will automatically have the rights.

If the book is your own and you hold the necessary rights for the content, select "This is not a public domain work and I hold the necessary publishing rights."

- Target your book to customers

There are many different categories on Amazon for your book to fall under, and in this section you will have the opportunity to select up to 2. In order to select the correct category, simply put yourself in the shoes of your readers. Which category would they need to search under in order to find your book? For example, my 'How2Become' books always fall under the category of "**careers**". Here's a step-by-step tutorial for choosing the correct category for your book.

Choose the main genre/category for your book - From the following list, select the main category your book falls under:

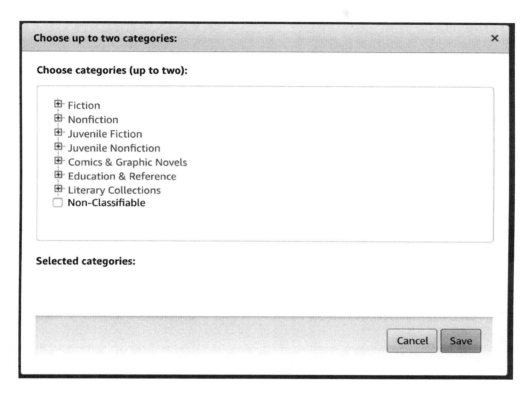

You will then see a drop-down menu appear for each category. For example, when I click **Nonfiction**, the following sub categories are available:

- Antiques & Collectibles

- Architecture

- Art

- Bibles

- Biography & Autobiography

- Body, Mind & Spirit

- Business & Economics

- Computers

- Cooking

❑ Crafts & Hobbies

❑ Design

❑ Drama

❑ Family & Relationships

❑ Games

❑ Gardening

❑ Health & Fitness

❑ History

❑ House & Home

❑ Humour

❑ Language Arts & Disciplines

❑ Law

❑ Literary Criticism

❑ Mathematics

❑ Medical

❑ Music

❑ Nature

❑ Performing Arts

❑ Pets

❑ Philosophy

❑ Photography

❑ Poetry

❑ Political Science

❑ Psychology

❑ Religion

❑ Science

❑ Self-Help

❑ Social Science

❑ Sports & Recreation

❑ Technology & Engineering

❑ Transportation

❑ Travel

❑ True Crime

I then need to drill down further to find my chosen category. From experience, I know that **Careers** falls under **Business & Economics**. When I select **Business & Economics** and scroll down, "**Careers**" appears:

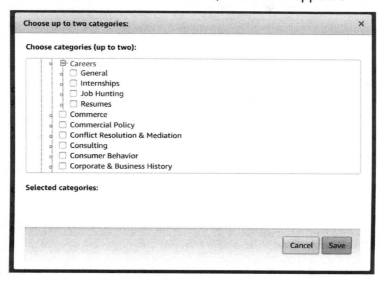

Finally, all I need to do now is choose the relevant sub category for **Careers** that is relevant to my book, and that happens to be **Job hunting**:

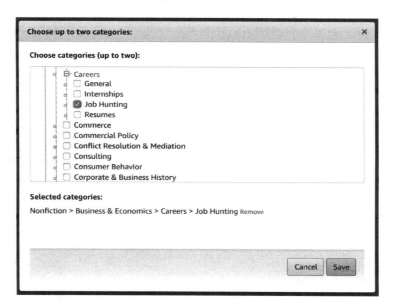

Amazon then confirms in the box that my selected category is:

Nonfiction > Business & Economics > Careers > Job Hunting

Don't forget, you actually get to do this twice, so make sure you choose 2 categories for your book!

- Search keywords (up to 7, optional)

When you add keywords, these will help your readers to find your book when they search the Kindle Store, so make sure you add them. You can enter keywords or short phrases that describe your book and are relevant to its content. The best keywords are those that do not repeat words in the title, category, or description, as these are currently already used to help readers find your book. Please note: Amazon does not accept search keywords that mislead or manipulate their customers. Examples of items that are prohibited as search keywords include but are not limited to:

- Reference to other authors;

- Reference to books by other authors;

- Reference to sales rank (i.e. 'bestselling');

- Reference to advertisements or promotions (i.e. 'free');

- Reference to anything that is unrelated to your book's content.

To give you an idea of the type of keywords I might include for a book, here is an example:

TITLE: How to Become a Firefighter

Keywords: Careers, interview questions, application forms, job hunting, psychometric tests, CV.

- Upload or create a book cover

This is the section where you get to upload the all-important book cover! Kindle Direct Publishing accepts only two types of files for cover images:

JPEG, or .jpeg

TIFF, or .tif(f)

KDP applies additional compression to images when displaying them on its website. For best results images should be uploaded with minimal compression.

Dimensions

Requirements for the size of your cover art have an ideal height/width ratio of 1.6, this means:

- A minimum of 625 pixels on the shortest side and 1000 pixels on the longest side

- For best quality, your image would be 1563 pixels on the shortest side and 2500 pixels on the longest side

Colour

Product images display on the Amazon website using RGB (red, green, blue) colour mode. Use colour images whenever possible and relevant. The Kindle reading device has a black and white screen today, but Kindle applications for other devices, such as iPhone or PC, take advantage of colour fonts and images.

Borders for White Cover Art

Cover art with white or very light backgrounds can seem to disappear against the white background. Adding a very narrow (3-4 pixel) border in medium grey will define the boundaries of the cover.

Now that your book is on sale in both Kindle and print formats, let's take a look at what it takes to become a bestselling author.

CHAPTER 17 –

Becoming A Bestselling Author – The Blueprint

So, those eagle-eyed readers amongst you will have noticed my book has the word 'bestselling' in the title. On that basis, I need to share with you some invaluable tips that will help you to achieve bestseller status. But before I come on to the tips, let's quickly look at what being a bestselling author actually means:

TO QUALIFY AS A BESTSELLING AUTHOR, YOUR BOOK MUST RANK IN THE TOP 100 OF ANY CATEGORY ON AMAZON.

Of course, you will probably now ask me how long does the book have to stay in that top 100 category for it to qualify as a bestseller? The answer is the book simply must rank in the top 100 of any category **once** for it to be a bestseller! Once your book achieves bestseller you can then use this 'status' in all future book marketing and promotion activities.

MY BLUEPRINT FOR ACHIEVING BESTSELLER STATUS

TIP 1 – Write fantastic content

If your book's content is weak, it will most probably fail to hit the bestseller spot. Whenever I sit down to write a book I always ask myself what the **transformation** will be once the reader has completed the content. For example, when planning the structure for this book, the transformation would be that the author could feasibly write and publish a bestselling book after reading and following the information I provide. Then, once I have established the transformation, I will write down the steps it takes a person to achieve the transformation. These steps are effectively the chapter titles. You will see that by defining a transformation for my book, which includes detailed step-by-step advice on how to achieve a goal, the reader is far more likely to enjoy the book and find it highly beneficial. If the reader loves the content, they will not only leave you a positive review, but they will also tell other people about the book, too.

TIP 2 – Make sure your book title and strapline are spot on

As you have gathered through previous chapters, the book title and strapline are very important in helping a book reach bestseller status. I spend lots of time thinking carefully about the title and strapline for my books to make sure they help the reader understand exactly what the content is about and how it will help them.

The second reason to make sure your book's title and strapline are spot on is with regards to online searches. For many of my books, they appear on the first page of Amazon for the relevant search terms. By getting the book title and strapline right, I am essentially putting my books under the noses of the people who are looking for that genre of content.

TIP 3 – Create a fantastic book cover design

If you walked into a car showroom with the intention of buying a second-hand car and you noticed the car you wanted to buy was dirty, not cleaned and not prepared for sale, how would you feel? Chances are, you wouldn't buy it! Despite it being the same car underneath the dirt with regards to design and performance, you wouldn't make the purchase. On the same basis, if a book cover design doesn't do the content justice, your customers will not buy it. Take the time and effort to create a brilliant book cover design and your chances of reaching bestseller status will skyrocket.

Here's a really cool tip for finding the best book cover designers on UpWork. com:

Go to Google and type in:

"Best Book Cover Designers Upwork"

You will then be presented with the following results:

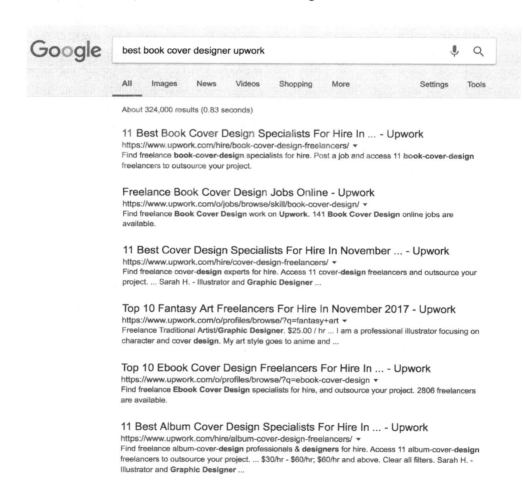

The very first search engine results page listing says:

"11 Best Book Cover Design Specialists for Hire"

Click on this link and it will take you through to a page on UpWork.com that lists the highest rated book cover designs for that particular month. You can choose which one from the 11 listed you want to work with based on your budget and personal preferences.

TIP 4 – Typeset the printed book for style!

When someone picks up your book, you want them to love how it looks, feels and how the content is presented. This can be achieved by using a great typesetter to prepare your book for the printing process. I have seen many negative reviews on other authors books whereby people are criticising the layout and presentation of the content. Don't cut corners by trying to typeset the book yourself; instead, pay a professional to do the work for you.

TIP 5 – Format the eBook for compatibility across all devices

There are so many different e-reading devices out there right now, such as the Amazon E-Reader, Amazon Paperwhite, Kindle Oasis, Kindle Voyage, inkBOOK, KOBO, BOOX, the list goes on! On that basis, it is very important your eBook is compatible across all devices. When you move onto the next chapter, you will notice that I encourage you to sell across multiple channels, including eBook channels. Therefore, your eBook needs to be compatible across all devices. The last thing you want to happen is to spend months writing your masterpiece, only for it to receive a negative review for poor eBook formatting. Again, using the advice I provided in the preceding tip, go to Google and search for "**Best eBook Conversion Upwork**" and you will undoubtedly find someone to do the work for you.

TIP 6 – Keywords in your book description

When you upload your book to Amazon you will have the opportunity to input the book's description. Again, make sure you get this bit right and include all the relevant details pertaining to your book. You should also consider including the chapter title for your book, to give your readers a good idea as to what type of content they are getting for their money.

There is another really cool tip I want to share with you whilst on this subject – **HTML code**. You will notice on some Amazon sales pages that the descriptive text contains bold text and line spacing. This type of formatting really helps the text to stand out on the page. Amazon only allows certain HTML code in descriptions. To help you, the following editor allows you to quickly and easily create description that match Amazon's criteria:

http://twoschmucks.com/amazon-description-editor/

TIP 7 – Get your categories right

In the previous chapter I provided details relating to Amazon categories and how you can choose 2 for your book. A browse category is the section of the Amazon site where users can find your book. Think of the browse category like the sections of a physical bookstore (fiction, history, and so on). You can select up to two browse categories for your book. Precise browse categorisation helps readers find your book.

First and foremost, be sure to choose 2 categories, because if you don't, Amazon will automatically choose them for you. You know your book subject best, so it makes sense you choose them. When choosing your categories, here's a great tip:

For the first category, choose one that's blatantly obvious. As in the previous chapter, you will see the first category for my 'How2Become' books I chose was:

Nonfiction > Business & Economics > Careers > Job Hunting

For the second category, I recommend you choose one that's a bit more niche/targeted. Preferably one where there might be fewer books listed. Most authors will categorise their books with two really obvious categories, and whilst this fine, their book will be competing with thousands of other books. If the second book category you choose is more niche, and as such less competitive, you will increase your chances of reaching bestseller. To give you an example, for my 'How2Become' series books, which contain interview questions and answers, I might opt for this second category:

Education & Reference > Reference > Questions & Answers

Don't underestimate the importance of both choosing and getting your categories right.

Finally, there is absolutely nothing wrong with trying different categories later down the line, once your book is published. If you are not happy with your sales, or if you haven't yet reached bestseller status, try choosing different categories.

TIP 8 – Pricing

As a new published author, it is very tempting to launch your book with a low price to tempt sales. Whilst it is entirely down to you how you price your book, here are some things to consider first:

- **Nonfiction** books generally sell for more than fiction or children's books.

- Regardless of how long a **fiction** book is, most readers will not pay more than £10 for a print copy and £7 for Kindle.

- **Children's books** are generally pitched under the £10, with many being sold for £7 or less.

- If you sell your book too cheaply, not only will you not make much profit each one sold, you will also give the impression the book is 'cheap'. If your content is strong, make sure you set the price accordingly.

- Remember to think about **perceived value** when setting the price for your book. Go too low and people will not consider the content to be worthy.

- If you are unsure as to what price to sell your book at, take a look at other similar books on Amazon and see what price they are selling for.

Whilst it is entirely down to you how much you sell your book for, here are some guidelines based on genre:

Nonfiction print – Between £9.99 and £15

Nonfiction Kindle – Between £5.99 and £7.50

Fiction print – Between £4.99 and £9.99

Fiction Kindle – Between £2.99 and £7.50

Children's print – Between £4.99 and £9.99

Children's Kindle – Between £2.99 and £7.50

TIP 10 – Create your Amazon Author Central page

Many authors do not create a dedicated author page on Amazon. I don't know about you, but whenever I buy a book from a new author, I want to know more about them before making my purchase. If the author hasn't created an author biography page, it is hard for me to get know more about them and their work – I want to see the author is real and I also want to read more about them before buying their work. Creating an author bio is fast and easy. All you need to do is head over to authorcentral.amazon.co.uk and sign up for your author page once there. At Author Central, you have the opportunity to share the most up-to-date information about yourself and your work with your readers -- you can view and edit your bibliography, add a photo and biography to a personal profile and upload missing book cover images. Once you create your author page, readers will be able to click the **+Follow** button to receive the latest news, updates and books that you release.

TIP 11 – Create a book promotional video for Amazon

I strongly believe this is another important aspect of the bestsellers blueprint. In addition to creating your Amazon Author Central page, create and upload a video that features either yourself or an actor giving a brief presentation about your book. The video only has to be one-minute in duration. The benefits of creating a book promotional video on Amazon are as follows:

- Readers will get to see you, the real person!

- A video enables you to 'connect' with your readers in a way that text can't achieve.

- During the video, you can explain what the book is about, including the storyline and/or key features and benefits of your book.

- You can hold up a copy of your book in the video and refer to specific sections or points of interest within the book.

- You can include a 'call to action' within the video. Basically, this is where you encourage your readers to buy your book on Amazon by simply saying – "Get your copy of my book right now and Amazon will deliver it to you within 24-hours".

For those people who are not confident enough to create their own video, or if you are writing under a pseudonym, consider using an actor on the website Fiverr.com. The following person comes highly recommended: www.fiverr.com/videosforall

TIP 12 – Promote and market your book

OK, so it's very easy for me to say to you – "Once your book is published, make sure you promote it!" However, giving you the right type of marketing advice is a different thing. There are so many ways you can market and promote your book nowadays, including YouTube, Facebook, Instagram, blogs, review websites, awards, Amazon Marketing Services etc. On that basis, I have dedicated and entire chapter to these and other methods towards the end of the book.

CHAPTER 18 –

Getting Your Book Stocked In Waterstones

GETTING YOUR BOOK STOCKED IN WATERSTONES

I have always said that one of the main reasons for my success in publishing is because I sell through multiple channels.

The first thing to stress is that in order to sell your physical books through many different channels, you will need to hold your own stock. The problem with holding onto lots of physical stock is that you need the space to achieve this, and this can cost you in terms of business rates for the extra square footage required. However, if you opt for digital printing then you will be able to keep sufficient stock to meet demand, without having to pay for expensive storage or office space. One other method to employ is to actually ask your printer to ship your printed book direct to your main distributors.

At the time of writing, I sell both physical and digital books to a variety of different book buyers, including Gardners.com, Bertram Books, Waterstones, eBay, independent book stores and hundreds of UK book sellers.

TO GET YOUR BOOK STOCKED IN WATERSTONES YOU MUST GET YOUR BOOK STOCKED WITH GARDNERS BOOKS (GARDNERS.COM)

Making use of a distributer to sell through multiple channels (Gardners. com)

A book distributer is an organisation who will stock your books on consignment basis (sale or return), and sell them to literally thousands of book retailers around the globe. The main reason why I choose to use a distributor is simply because I don't want the hassle and expense of having to make contact with all of the book retailers myself. Whilst there are a few other book distributors across the UK, I personally choose Gardners.com. As mentioned above, to get your book stocked in Waterstones you must get your book stocked with Gardners Books.

About Gardners Books

Gardners Books is 'Britain's Leading Book Wholesaler', and the supplier of choice for thousands of booksellers and retailers around the world. As a publisher, you can take advantage of this by stocking or listing your titles with them. Gardners provides a one-stop shop for any book retailer, with the widest range of stock titles available in the UK. For you as the publisher, this provides you with instant access to over 15,000 retailers across the UK and overseas.

Whilst Gardners do take a large cut (negotiable), I have always found them extremely efficient, helpful and conscientious. In a nutshell, whenever I publish a new book I will send Gardners an **Advanced Trade Information** sheet (ATI), which will also include an image of the book cover. They will then upload the details of the book onto their system so that book retailers can order them direct from Gardners. When a book retailer orders stock direct from Gardners, Gardners will send the books direct to them based on minimum order levels. The retailer will then sell the books for a profit. There is no guarantee Gardners will take your book. To try and get your book stocked with Gardners.com, you will need to apply for a publisher's account.

How to get your books stocked with Gardners

The set of criteria that you must meet to get your books stocked, is as follows:

1) All publishers must be registered with Nielsen and have a valid ISBN including a visible barcode (most commonly on the bottom right of the back cover). You can find out more about obtaining ISBN numbers here:

www.nielsenisbnstore.com

As previously covered, you can download a free barcode generator software tool at:

www.nchsoftware.com/barcode/

2) For stock titles the publisher must have UK Representation, and the stock must be available from a UK location. It is acceptable for yourself, as the publisher, to be the representative, providing your stock is located in the UK.

3) To qualify as a stock line, printed books must be available.

If your title(s) do meet the above criteria, then you will then need to send Gardners a sample copy for review to the following address, ensuring that they are clearly labelled as 'samples'. Please note: Gardners will not return samples or acknowledge receipt.

FAO Buyers New Publishers,

Buying Office,

Gardners Books,

1 Whittle Drive,

Eastbourne,

East Sussex

BN23 6QH.

What Happens Next?

Gardners will contact you if they decide to stock your books. Where it is agreed to stock books, Gardners will then discuss commercial terms with you as the publisher. Almost without exception, books from new publisher relationships will be taken into stock on a consignment basis (i.e. they hold stock and pay monthly on sales achieved). Other commercial terms (e.g. discount levels) will also be agreed.

If you have not heard from Gardners within four weeks, this will mean they have decided not to hold your books in stock at this time. One way to improve your chances of Gardners taking on your books, is to provide them with any previous sales records. For example, when I first approached Gardners to sell my books for me, I sent them an entire six month sales sheets, from sales generated both on Amazon and through my own website. I also offered to give them 60% discount off the recommend list price – I am sure this helped with their decision to stock my books.

Advanced Trade Information sheets

Advance Trade Information Sheets (ATIs), or simply AIs, should be sent four months before each title is produced, and they should be supplied by the publisher to the wholesaler and sales representatives, key accounts, overseas agents, and anyone else in the trade who might be interested in the book.

The AI should normally contain the following:

- Publisher's logo;

- Name of author(s), editor, illustrator, as appropriate;

- Title and sub-title, and series title where relevant;

- Publication date;

- Suggested retail price;

- ISBN;

- Number of pages and illustrations;

- Format and binding(s);

- Language;

- Two or three key selling points;

- Brief summary of contents, indicating localities where relevant;

- Brief details of the author(s) or editor: including where they are from and where they live;

- Intended readership;

- Promotional details: serialisation, press, TV & radio features, launches, etc.;

- Reviews and recommendations: brief quotations from respected, named sources;

- Cover, author photograph or other appropriate image;

- Publisher's contact details;

- Distributors' contact details.

Here is a sample ATI to give you a better idea of what one looks like:

SAMPLE ADVANCED TRADE INFORMATION SHEET

Suite 14, 50 Churchill Square, Kings Hill, Kent. ME19 4YU

Contact Email Address: info@How2Become.co.uk

Publishers Website Address www.How2Become.com

(Jacket Illustration)

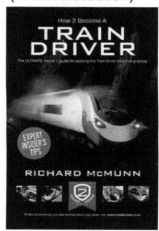

Title: How To Become A Train Driver: The insider's guide

ISBN 9781909229501

Author/Illustrator- Richard McMunn

Size in mm - 19.4 x 12.8 x 10 mm

Pages -160

Binding - Paperback

Age – Adult

Publication Date – 14th January 2014

SYNOPSIS:

HOW TO BECOME A TRAIN DRIVER: THE INSIDER'S GUIDE

Want to become a Train Driver? There are more candidates than ever, but this INSIDER'S guide will help you get the career you want. The selection process for becoming a Train Driver includes a requirement to complete an application form, attend an assessment day, and pass two interviews.

This comprehensive guide will take you through the entire selection process and help you to secure this fantastic career at the first attempt. The selection process is highly competitive, but there a number of things you can do in order to increase your chances of success.

This guide contains:

- Tips on completing a successful application;
- Sample responses to the application form questions;
- Tips on how to prepare for the assessment day;
- Sample Concentration tests;
- Advice on the new train driver tests and how to pass them;
- Insider tips on how to pass the interviews;
- Sample interview questions;
- Responses to the interview questions to help you prepare.

KEY SALES POINTS:

- Contains insider tips and advice from industry experts
- Provides sample interview questions and responses
- Provides advice for passing the NEW train driver tests
- Lots of sample testing questions

Richard McMunn is a former serving Fire Officer and now founder, creator and owner of the How2Become.com careers website.

How2Become.com is the UK's leading careers information website. We go to great lengths to find the right people to create our products. Sometimes, we even put a member of our team through a particular selection process so that we can find out exactly what it takes to pass. Visit www.How2Become. com for more guides, products and training courses to help you succeed.

DISTRIBUTED BY: How2Become Ltd

Distributors full address: Suite 1, 60 Churchill Square, Kings Hill, Kent. ME19 4YU

RRP: £13.00

Contact: How2Become Ltd

Telephone No: 07890 XXX XXX

Email address: info@How2Become.co.uk

Website address: www.How2Become.com

Getting your book into Waterstones and other High Street stores

Waterstones buy all their books from small publishers via Gardners. Therefore, to get your book(s) listed in Waterstones, both online and in store, you will need to apply for an account. In order to sell to the Waterstones branches, it is necessary to register with Waterstones via Gardners. To do this you will need to contact the **Independent Publisher Coordinator** by email: ipc@ waterstones.com and ask for a 'Waterstones Trading Application Form'.

Once the form is completed, you then need to return the form to Gardners, as explained on the form. Once you are registered, Waterstones will notify you that you may market your books to their branches.

When a branch of Waterstones orders copies of your books, the orders go direct to Gardners, who in turn order from you or your distributor. The book is then delivered to Gardners, who will supply the branches with the product.

IMPORTANT NOTE: Waterstones will not accept deliveries direct to store, they must come via Gardners Books.

My view on selling your books through Waterstones

Purely from a business perspective, I do not put much effort into selling my books in Waterstones stores. Not only do my books sell far better on Amazon, but I have also found Waterstones difficult to deal with on occasions. This may simply be down to the fact that Waterstones cannot compete with Amazon prices in my particular niche area of careers related books. Alternatively, it's worth nothing that Waterstones do have a sustained bias towards fiction books. While they still sell non-fiction guides, ultimately it's the fiction books that make them the most money, and as such these are the books that you generally see in the front window of the Waterstones stores. So, you might have better luck persuading Waterstones to sell a fiction book than a non-fiction book.

My advice would certainly be to try and get your books on sale in Waterstones stores. After all, every additional sale is worth the effort! Please be aware that all the marketing for your book will be down to you, the publisher.

CHAPTER 19 –

How To Protect Your Intellectual Property & Book Disclaimers

HOW TO PROTECT YOUR INTELLECTUAL PROPERTY & BOOK DISCLAIMERS

One of the first and most important rules as an author and self-publisher is to protect your intellectual property.

As an author and self-publisher, you will constantly be watching your competitors and trying to close the door on any 'holes in your business' that people could potentially exploit. For example, when I started writing my first book under the brand name 'How2Become' I immediately looked at ways to protect the name. I felt that it was a strong/unique name, and therefore I wanted to protect it. Using some of the early profits I was making from selling my guides, I decided to apply for the trademark 'How2Become'. It took me many months to get the trademark, but it was a very wise move.

Whilst obtaining a trademark can be a lengthy and expensive process, it is certainly worth the effort and the additional cost, especially if you have a strong brand or idea. The **National Business Register** is an excellent source for protecting your business name against 'passing off' and other common problems.

VISIT: www.start.biz

You will also want to protect your intellectual property by way of copyright. The purpose of copyright is to allow creators (authors) to gain economic rewards for their efforts, and so encourage future creativity and the development of new material, which benefits us all. Copyright material is usually the result of creative skill and/or significant labour and/or investment, and without protection it would often be very easy for others to exploit material without paying the creator. There is no official registration system for copyright in the UK and most other parts of the world, as registration is not needed.

There are no forms to fill in and no fees to pay to get copyright protection, as under a number of international conventions it is automatically granted to the creator of a copyrightable work. This means that as soon as you create a work which falls into one of the categories of material that qualifies for copyright protection, you will have copyright, without having to do anything further to establish your claim.

However, copyright owners (authors) can take certain precautions to help establish their rights. A copy of your work could be deposited with a bank or solicitor. Alternatively, an author could send himself or herself a copy of their manuscript by special delivery post (which gives a clear date stamp on the envelope), leaving the envelope unopened on its return. You may also decide to simply email your manuscript to yourself by way of an attachment – this will provide proof that you actually owned the rights to the work, on the date the email was sent. If you feel that it will take you many months or even years to finish your manuscript, simply send yourself each chapter as and when it is completed.

Whatever you do, make sure you take the time to protect your business environment and your intellectual property. You can find free and impartial advice with regard to copyright law, trademarks and patents at the following website:

www.ipo.gov.uk

There are many companies and solicitors out there who will charge you a considerable fee to protect your copyright. Whilst there is nothing wrong with taking this approach (providing you have the funds available), my advice would be to simply protect your IP for free using one of the methods described earlier in this section.

Non-disclosure and confidentiality agreements

Think very carefully about disclosing your book idea to others before you have obtained protection for it. Disclosure can also invalidate your ability to apply for protection. In many cases a third party will agree to sign a non-disclosure or confidentiality agreement (NDA). For example, whenever I coach my students during my one-to-one coaching programme at **www. RichardMentorMe.com**, I will always sign an NDA if the client asks me to.

Copyright page to insert in your book

It is a good idea to include a copyright page at the start of your book that asserts your rights as the owner of the intellectual property.

Below is a sample copyright page that is often used in books:

Assignment of copyright notices

On a few very rare occasions, I have employed an outsourcer (ghost-writer) to write specialist books for my publishing business. Before we agree a fee for the work, I also state very clearly that they must sign an **'assignment of copyright notice'** once the work is completed. This notice is also sometimes referred to as a 'Transfer of copyright' agreement.

This assignment of copyright form basically assigns the rights of the written work to me once I have paid the agreed fee. This form then provides proof that I actually own the rights to the intellectual property that they have written, and that they have no rights to the work at any time in the future. The reason why I ask a ghost-writer to sign the form is that I do not want them approaching me at any time during the future to ask for royalty payments.

The following is an example of an assignment of copyright notice for a book which you can use. Please ensure that you take legal advice before using it as I cannot be held responsible for its content or any issues that arise from its use:

ASSIGNMENT OF COPYRIGHT (EXAMPLE ONLY)

This Assignment of Copyright (the "Assignment") is made and entered on the DATE GOES HERE, by and between XXXXXX ("Author") and XXXXXX ("Assignee") (collectively referred to as the "Parties").

Whereas,

i. The Author is the sole creator and owner of **NAME OF THE WRITTEN WORKS GOES HERE** and

ii. The Author wishes to assign his/her copyright to Assignee.

Now, therefore, for valuable consideration, receipt and sufficiency of which are hereby acknowledged, the Parties agree as follows:

1. ASSIGNMENT: In consideration of **NAME OF THE WRITTEN WORKS GOES HERE** by Assignee to Author, Author hereby assigns, sells and transfers to Assignee all of his/her rights, title and interest in and to the Work, including, but not limited to: (i) all rights under copyright for the full legal term of copyright and all renewals, extensions, revisions and revivals together with all accrued rights of action throughout the world in any form and in any language (including all media, both now known or later developed) and any registrations and copyright applications relating thereto, and (ii) all income, royalties or claims relating to the Work due on or after the date of this Assignment.

2. AUTHOR'S REPRESENTATIONS: Author represents and warrants that he/she is the sole creator and owner of the Work, and has all rights, title and interest in and to the copyright in the Work and the power to enter into this Assignment. Author further represents and warrants that the rights transferred in this Assignment are free of lien, encumbrance or adverse claim.

3.   FURTHER ASSURANCES: Author will co-operate fully to do all such further acts and things and execute or sign any further documents, instruments, notices or consents as may be reasonable and necessary or desirable to give full effect to the arrangements contemplated by this Agreement.

4.   BINDING EFFECT: The covenants and conditions contained in this Assignment shall apply to and bind the Parties and their heirs, legal representatives, successors and permitted assigns.

5. GOVERNING LAW: This Assignment shall be governed by and construed in accordance with the laws of England and Wales. Any disputes arising from matters relating to this Agreement shall be exclusively subject to the jurisdiction of the courts of England and Wales.

IN WITNESS WHEREOF, the Parties have caused this Assignment to be executed on the day and year first above written.

AUTHOR:

XXXXXX

Date and sign

ASSIGNEE:

XXXXXXX

Date and sign

The use of images on your book covers or website

When you have your first book cover or website created, you will undoubtedly want to add some images to it. Whatever you do, make sure you obtain a licence to use your chosen images. Some people think they can go online, search for images in Google and then simply use them freely on a commercial basis – this is untrue. I am aware of some authors and entrepreneurs who have been fined for using images on their website without permission. Do not just take images from the Internet and use them on your website unless you are 100% sure they are free to use. My advice is to use a **royalty-free stock image website** and pay for the licence to use the image(s). The fees in order to use the images are relatively cheap!

The safest way to find 'royalty free' images with appropriate licences is to pay for their use on 'image stock' websites such as:

www.istockphoto.com

www.gettyimages.co.uk

www.fotolia.com

www.shutterstock.com

www.bigstockimages.com

www.123RF.com

You should be able to find the images that you need for your book cover or website at any of the above websites, but be sure to check the licences first to ensure that they are suitable for commercial use. If you can't use the image, there will generally be a warning sign in the description, saying 'For editorial use only' or words to that effect.

If you need to find images to use that are more niche, you might find them at the following website:

www.photographersdirect.com

Here's one final thing with regards to use of images on book covers and on websites. If you are using images on your website, then you should opt for a maximum image size of **72dpi**. Using images which have a higher resolution than this can slow the speed of your website down considerably! However, if you are using images for book covers, then they will need to be a minimum of **300dpi and 1000 pixels in quality** to ensure good results during reproduction and print.

How to check that ghost-written work is unique

I often get asked by authors how they can check whether or not a piece of ghost-written work they have paid for is actually unique, and not simply copied or plagiarised from a 3rd party. Copyscape.com is a free plagiarism checker. The software lets you detect duplicate content and check if your articles are original:

www.CopyScape.com

Book disclaimers

You may decide to include a disclaimer in your book. To assist you, the following are some of the more common ones used within different book genres:

MY DISCLAIMER - I do not assume and hereby disclaim any liability to any party for any loss, damage, or disruption caused by errors or omissions, whether such errors or omissions result from negligence, accident, or any other cause by using any of the disclaimers within this section. Please ensure you take proper legal advice before using any of the following disclaimers.

(memoir)

Some names and identifying details/information have been changed to protect the privacy of individuals.

(fiction, novels, mystery, crime and thrillers and short stories)

This book is a work of fiction. Names, characters, businesses, places, events and incidents are either the products of the author's imagination or used in a fictitious manner. Any resemblance to actual persons, living or dead, or actual events is purely coincidental.

(memoir, autobiography)

In order to maintain their anonymity, in some instances, I have changed the names of individuals and places. I may have changed some identifying characteristics and details such as physical properties, occupations and places of residence.

(advice, self-help and how-to)

Although the author and publisher have made every effort to ensure that the information in this book was correct at the time of publication, the author and publisher do not assume and hereby disclaim any liability to any party for any loss, damage, or disruption caused by errors or omissions, whether such errors or omissions result from negligence, accident, or any other cause.

(health, alternative healing)

This book is not intended as a substitute for the medical advice of physicians. The reader should regularly consult a physician in matters relating to his/her health and particularly with respect to any symptoms that may require diagnosis or medical attention.

(sports, training)

The information in this book is meant to supplement, not replace, proper (name your sport) training. Like any sport involving speed, equipment, balance and environmental factors, (this sport) poses some inherent risk. The authors and publisher advise readers to take full responsibility for their safety, know their limits and take advice from a qualified medical professional practitioner before carrying out any of the exercises within this book. Before practicing the skills described in this book, be sure that your equipment is well maintained, and do not take risks beyond your level of experience, aptitude, training, and comfort level.

CHAPTER 20 –
Using Outsourcers

USING OUTSOURCERS

For your book to achieve profitability quickly, you will need to keep your production costs to an absolute minimum. Whether you are getting your book cover created, getting your manuscript converted to Kindle, or getting a website built to promote your book(s), you will naturally want to keep your costs down whilst maintaining quality.

The title of this book, 'How to write and publish a bestselling book', aims to teach you how to make your writing and publishing ventures profitable, and it is this particular chapter that will help you to do just that. One of the main reasons why I manage to generate 6-figure net profits year in, year out, is because I am highly-effective at outsourcing.

> "SUCCESSFUL OUTSOURCING WILL NOT ONLY ALLOW YOU TO FOCUS ON WHAT YOU DO BEST, WRITING THE CONTENT, BUT IT WILL ALSO HELP YOU TO FIND OTHER WAYS TO PROMOTE YOUR BOOK AND EXPAND YOUR RANGE OF TITLES. BY BUILDING RELATIONSHIPS WITH YOUR OUTSOURCERS THAT ARE BASED ON TRUST AND RESPECT YOU WILL BE ABLE TO CREATE A PUBLISHING TEAM THAT CAN ACCOMPLISH JUST ABOUT ANYTHING...AND GIVE YOU MUCH DESERVED TIME-OFF IN THE PROCESS."

The official definition of outsourcing is as follows:

'To obtain (goods or a service) from an outside supplier, in place of an internal source.'

I personally prefer to define outsourcing as:

'To obtain (goods or a service) from an outside supplier to MASSIVELY increase the profits in your publishing business.'

Whenever I publish a book I will always aim to make it as profitable as possible. I want you to do the same!

The pros and cons of outsourcing

There are many advantages to using outsourcers, which I will list below:

✓ There is a massive pool of talent out there in the world today, all at your fingertips.

✓ You can outsource literally everything within your writing and publishing business!

✓ Outsourcers allow you to concentrate on what <u>you</u> are GOOD at, and also what you ENJOY doing.

✓ You don't have to speak to or ever meet the outsourcers.

✓ Outsourcing can be very cost-effective, which means more money in your pocket.

✓ Outsourcing can triple or even quadruple your profits.

✓ The cost of living in many countries outside of the UK or US is far lower – therefore, the cost of outsourcing is a lot cheaper, too.

✓ There are some really good outsourcers for you to tap in to.

✓ Outsourcers can work whilst you are asleep due to the time difference.

✓ If an outsourcer cannot work due to sickness or holiday, they don't get paid.

✓ When you hire full or part-time staff within your business, you are bound by employment and other laws within the UK. When you hire outsourcers you are only bound by the terms and conditions of the website from which you hire them from and your own contract (which you control) between yourself and the outsourcer.

There are also a number of disadvantages to outsourcing too:

✗ There are so many outsourcers and outsourcing websites out there that it is hard to determine who is genuine and who is not.

✗ It can be confusing, unless you know what you are doing.

✗ It is hard to let go and trust people with your work, especially if you are not going to meet the outsourcer or even speak to them.

✗ Outsourcers can potentially damage or even ruin your business.

✗ It can be difficult to communicate with them if their English is not very good.

✗ Unless you provide the outsourcer with a solid brief and explain exactly what it is you want doing, things can go wrong.

Although the disadvantages do put many people off using outsourcers, my advice is to give it a try and see how you get on, as it can be extremely advantageous. During the following sections I will teach you how to outsource for success.

What can I outsource?

With regards to writing and publishing books, you can outsource just about everything, from writing the content for all or part of a book, through to typesetting and Kindle conversion. Here is a list of just some of the areas you can outsource within a publishing business:

o   Book writing;

o   Book cover design;

o   Logo creation and branding;

o   Proofreading/editing;

o   Typesetting;

o   Printing;

o   Customer service/care;

o   eBook/Kindle conversion;

o   Website sales-copy;

o   Advertising/marketing and Public Relations (PR);

o   Website design/development;

o   Social media management;

o   Google and other search engine pay-per-click advertising;

o   Search engine optimisation.

Although I write my own books 99% of the time, I do sometimes come up with book ideas where I feel that I do not have sufficient knowledge or expertise in the subject area to do the content justice. As a result I will need to find a competent and proficient ghost-writer to create the content on my behalf.

Where to find outsourcers

There are many outsourcing companies available online for you to choose from. However, I recommend you only use the following 4 websites:

- Upwork.com

- 99Designs.com

- Fiverr.com

- PeoplePerHour.com

Whilst there are many outsourcing websites to choose from, I only ever use the above four. Here is what I use each of these outsourcing websites for within my publishing business:

Upwork.com – Typesetting, Kindle conversion, book cover design, website design and website coding/development, Google Pay-Per-Click AdWords management, social media ad management.

99Designs.co.uk – Book cover design and logo design.

Fiverr.com – the creation of web-based videos to help promote my books and services and also logo design.

PeoplePerHour.com – Basic admin and research tasks.

Of course, the choice is yours with regards to which outsourcing website(s) you choose, but if you are looking for just one website that will offer you a place to outsource everything, then I recommend Upwork.com.

An alternative great place to get your book cover design created

As mentioned above, www.99Designs.co.uk is a place where I go to on occasions to get my book cover designs created. It is slightly different from a standard outsourcing website, in the fact that lots of designers will create your book cover or logo for you based on your brief, and then you decide which one you like. The designer you choose will end up being the one who wins your money! Here's a more detailed explanation as to how it works:

STEP 1 - Build a design brief for the designers to work from

First, you need to tell the designers what you want in your design. To do this, you will need to answer the questions in 99designs.co.uk's simple online brief.

STEP 2 - Choose a design package

The next step is to choose from one of four different design packages, which are clearly explained on their website. Once you have chosen a package you pay upfront, before 99designs.co.uk then launches your contest in their marketplace. A higher price will mean a bigger designer prize for the chosen designer, which means you will get more designers competing for your prize!

STEP 3 - Receive dozens of designs

Once the contest is launched, designers then get to work before submitting their designs directly to your account. You can log in each day to view the new designs.

STEP 4 – Provide feedback to the designers

You will have the opportunity to give feedback to your designers, so that you get the EXACT book cover design you want. You have the option to use ratings, comments and private messages to help designers shape their ideas to your needs. The more detailed your feedback, the easier it will be to get the design for your book that you really want.

STEP 5 - Pick the winner

After 7 days has passed, you need to pick the winner before signing the copyright agreement. 99Designs.co.uk will then transfer the prize money to the designer, before you download your new design and use it however you like.

How to outsource successfully

The first step to outsourcing success is to decide what exactly you want to outsource within your publishing business. To achieve this, I will write a list of things that I am not particular good at – this list will usually be the list of tasks that I end up outsourcing. Here's what my list will look like:

List of tasks I need to outsource

Book cover design;

Book typesetting;

eBook conversion;

Website design and sales copy;

Proofreading and editing;

Google Pay-Per-Click AdWords management.

Once I have compiled my list, I will then choose an outsourcing website on which to post my jobs. For example's sake, let's assume I want to publish a book called 'How to climb Mount Everest', but I do not have any expertise or knowledge of the subject.

Once I have opened my Upwork.com account, I will then post the following job:

TITLE – Competent and professional writer required for 'how to' guide.

I am seeking a highly competent and professional English author to write a 25,000-work book entitled 'How To Climb Mount Everest'. The book must consist of the following chapters:

- About Mount Everest
- Why do people climb it?
- The risks associated with climbing Mount Everest
- Mental state vs. physical state
- Preparing to climb
- Equipment you will need
- Financing your trip
- Base camp
- Advanced base camp
- Camp 1
- Camp 2
- Camp 3
- Camp 4 and Entering the Death-Zone
- Summit Day
- You're only half way there at the top!
- Useful links and resources

IMPORTANT NOTES:

1. The work must be unique, genuine and not copied from any websites or otherwise.

2. The content must be written in English as it is aimed predominantly at the UK market.

3. Upon completion of the project you will be required to sign a transfer of copyright agreement which transfers the copyright and intellectual property of the works over to me.

4. I require the completed written document to be supplied in Microsoft Word, font Arial and size 12, with 1.5 paragraph spacing.

5. The final deliverable written works must be delivered within 8 weeks.

6. The written works must be free from errors.

Whenever you upload a job to an outsourcing website, make sure your job brief details exactly what you want, down to the smallest detail. You will see in my job post that I have included 6 important notes. These enable me to have full control over the project, and they also ensure that I will not run into problems later down the line. When writing your job post, you need to assume that the outsourcer does not know anything about your job or what you want. Make sure you 'spoon feed' the outsourcers.

Now I will provide you with a sample outsourcing job post for a book cover designer:

> **TITLE – Competent and professional designer required to create book cover.**
>
> I am seeking an experienced, professional and competent designer to create a book cover for me based on the following details:
>
> - The book size will be 242mm x 170mm x 12mm spine.
>
> - I require the designer to supply all royalty free commercial use images for the cover as part of the cost.
>
> - I require a hi-resolution 300dpi front book image cover and a full hi-resolution jacket cover (print-ready) as part of the price.
>
> - You will be required to add a barcode and ISBN number to the artwork, which will be supplied by me.
>
> - You will be required to sign a transfer of copyright agreement upon completion of the design which hands over full copyright of the works to me.
>
> - The title and description for the book cover will be supplied once the successful candidate is selected.

You will note that I have not provided specific details of what the book subject is about at this stage. The reason for this is because I do not want anyone on the outsourcing website to see or steal my book idea. Once I have chosen the book cover designer, I will then provide that particular individual with a full brief relating to the title of the book cover.

You will notice that I did not hold back the book title and chapters within the ghost-writer job post. This was simply because I am looking for a particular specialist ghost-writer, who is capable of writing this type of content, and therefore I need to be specific from the outset.

My top tips for successful outsourcing

TIP #1 - DO NOT choose an outsourcer solely on price

"Some of the best outsourcers cost only slightly more than the cheapest..."

This is your business/future, so choose your outsourcers very carefully. People tend to jump in with both feet and take the first/cheapest person who comes along. This is often a mistake. Take the time to look at the outsourcer's credentials, experience, reviews, and previous work. When it comes to design work, you might also get a chance to look at their portfolio before making a decision. I recently hired a designer from Upwork based solely on her portfolio. Even though she barely had any hours of working on the site, I took one look at her portfolio and noticed that the work was of extremely good quality. Thus, I took a chance on her, and the results have been tremendous.

TIP #2 - Develop and use systems

> *"Without the use of outsourcing systems, you will fail."*

Your system must include:

- A system for getting the BEST outsourcers.

- What you want your outsourcers to do for you, and by when!

- How you want the work to be done.

- An agreed price/payment system.

- Agreed terms and conditions.

Remember to spoon feed the outsourcers – don't just assume that they know what you want them to create for you.

TIP #3 - Use <u>ONLY</u> the best outsourcers

> *"Outsourcing is BIG business now, and lots of people are bidding for your cash – choose your outsourcers very carefully."*

Ways to get the best outsourcers:

Use the most popular outsourcing websites, but do take care. (Upwork.com, 99Designs.co.uk, Fiverr.com and PeoplePerHour.com).

Check feedback and reviews of all the outsourcers you are considering hiring.

Be on the lookout for recommendations. Some of my most cherished outsourcers have come from recommendations.

Consider getting a mentor and use their outsourcers. For example, if you join my Author Mentoring Programme you will get access to all my outsourcers! Find out more at **www.RichardMentorMe.com**.

TIP #4 - Pay your outsourcers fast!

"I usually get a faster/better service because I always pay on time."

The aim is to build a strong working relationship with your outsourcers that will last for many years. By paying them promptly, you will get a better and faster service. Believe it or not, I only use a handful of outsourcers at any one time.

TIP #5 - Test your outsourcers before you agree to use them

"There are so many outsourcers out there, who are all competing for your business, that it can be hard to determine who is the best and has your best interests at heart."

Ways to test your outsourcers:

- Request an 'action-point' in the job description for those who apply. For example, I sometimes ask people to contact me using a reference number such as 'JOB2017'. Those people who contact me without making reference to the number have clearly not read my brief and will therefore not get hired!

- Consider trying out an outsourcer on a DIFFERENT task to the one you really want them to do (max. 1 hour).

- Keep tight control over the outsourcer's 'hours' in the early stages until you can trust them 100%.

- If you are paying an outsourcer to typeset your book, ask them to typeset a few pages initially, so you can see the type of work they are capable of producing.

TIP #6 - For larger, more complex jobs, consider using video to explain your brief

"Consider creating a short video tutorial to explain exactly what you want the outsourcer to do."

- Using a video tutorial for more complex job requests will ensure that no stone gets left unturned.

- You can use a tool such as **Camtasia Techsmith** (www.techsmith.com) to record a simple PowerPoint presentation.

- One of the most important elements of subcontracting is making sure that you and the subcontractor are on the same page, and that there are no surprises.

TIP #7 - Negotiate support for after the job is complete

"Once the job is complete and you have made your payment, you need to have the opportunity to go back to the outsourcer if required – a good outsourcer will not have a problem with this."

- Negotiate ongoing support after the work is completed. I usually ask for 7 days' support after a designer has created a book cover design or formatted/typeset my manuscript. This enables me to go back for minor changes if needed, and it also ensures that the outsourcer gets paid promptly, too.

- This is especially important for web development based projects.

- Agree a timeframe for the outsourcer to respond to all support requests.

TIP #8 - Don't pay for the job upfront unless using escrow

"Paying for a job in full upfront gives you no protection. The outsourcer may not stick to the agreed time-frame if you have already paid them for the job in advance."

- Negotiate an upfront fee to be paid in advance – usually 50%.

- If you use an outsourcing website or platform, you will need to pay the money into a holding account – this may sometimes be via escrow.

- Only release the money when you are 100% happy with the work, unless you have negotiated ongoing support.

TIP #9 - Clarify the ownership of the work when negotiating the deal

"It is very important that you negotiate the ownership of the work in advance. You want to have ownership to the copyright of the works, especially when outsourcing writing of books and articles etc."

- You can get caught out months or even years down the line if you do not verify the ownership of the intellectual property.

- Make sure you own the copyright or intellectual property relating to the works before agreeing a contract.

- A simple email confirming that you own the IP may suffice: "Can you please confirm that I will own the copyright/intellectual property to all elements of the work once completed and full payment has been made?"

- Insist on a **Transfer of Copyright Agreement** for books which are ghost-written.

TIP #10 - Leave positive feedback where credit is due

"I take great pride in the fact that I have excellent relationships with ALL my outsourcers. Very rarely do I receive work which is not to an outstanding level of quality."

- Remember to think about the future. You are looking to have a small team of outsourcers, who you can go back to time and time again.

- Many people forget to give credit when it is due. If the work is good, say so.

- I have a small number of outstanding outsourcers that do all of my work. I get priority treatment from my outsourcers.

- Here's what I might write in the feedback section of my outsourcer, if the work has been good: *"As usual, the work was carried out to a very high standard. XXXX is great to work with and always on-time. I would recommend her to anyone."*

CHAPTER 21 -
How To Market And Promote Your Book

HOW TO MARKET AND PROMOTE YOUR BOOK

In this next section of the guide, I will provide you with a number of useful methods for promoting and marketing your book. I have personally found that these methods have worked for me over the years, and you may decide to choose one or a number of them when developing and growing your own writing and publishing business.

#1 – About The Author

Check out the website www.AboutTheAUthor.co.uk and upload your book there. It's a free service that gives you exposure for your book.

#2 – Local Radio Stations

Local radio stations are a great place to promote your book. You have nothing to lose by sending a copy of your book off to radio stations and asking them if they would consider interviewing you about the book subject and the journey you have been on during the writing and publishing process. You can find a full list of UK-based radio stations at http://radiomap.eu/uk/

#3 – Hospital Radio Stations

Again, hospital radio stations are great place to get exposure for your book by way of an interview. A full list of hospital radio stations can be found at www.hbauk.com/member-stations

#4 – Competitions

Consider running a competition whereby the winner gets a free signed copy of your book. Websites such as www.woobox.com and www.rafflecopter.com are great for running competitions.

#5 – Book Review Blogs

A full list of book review blogs for you to contact can be found at the following website:

http://blog.feedspot.com/bookreview_blogs/

#6 – Book Launch Party

A great way to celebrate the launch of your book is to hold a book launch party/signing. Virtually all the authors who finish my VIP Author Mentoring Programme end up holding a book launch party, either at a local pub or their local Waterstones store. The benefit of holding the book launch party at your local pub is there will normally be no cost to hold the event. The pub gets the benefit of people buying drinks and nibbles, and you get somewhere warm and sociable to hold your party. Here are a couple of tips when preparing for your book lunch party:

- Send invitations out at least 4 weeks in advance to give people plenty of notice.

- A few days before the book launch party, contact all the attendees to remind them about the event.

- In my experience, the best time to hold the book launch party is at 7pm, mid-week.

- Make sure you have plenty of printed books at the event to sell. For example, authors who enrol onto my VIP Author Mentoring Programme receive 100 printed copies of their book. Those who hold a book launch party will usually sell all those books at the event.

- People will ask you to sign their copy of your book, so be prepared to do a few book signings!

- Take photos of people at the event holding your book and publish them on social media.

- Ask people at the book launch party to review your book on Amazon.

- Consider getting a roller banner created that acts as a focal point for your book party. Try the website **www.print-junction.co.uk** for a great roller banner creation service.

#7 – Press Release

Try creating a press release and send it off along with a copy of your book to the local press and media. Make sure you attach a covering letter asking the press and media to contact you for an interview. Be sure to give them your email address and your mobile phone contact, so they can get hold of you quickly. You can also create a press release at the website http://uk.prweb.com/.

#8 – Do a talk at your local school, college or university

I have done this before quite a few times and it gives you fantastic exposure, providing of course, your content is suitable and relevant for the pupils/students. You could even offer to give some of your books away to the school for free, in exchange for a bit of social media exposure on the school's social media channels.

#9 – Tell your first school you are now an author!

Once you become a published author, contact your secondary school and tell them about your book. Not only might the school ask you to go along to do a talk to the pupils, they might even add you to their website. The secondary school I attended, Balshaw's High School, has a dedicated page about me on their website. Remember, if you don't ask, you don't get!

#10 – Guest-posting

Guest-posting is where you contact websites in your niche and offer to write an interesting article that is focused on your books subject matter. This is a great, free way to gain exposure. I have carried out lots of guest-blogging in my time and I have gained valuable exposure for my books and my business.

#11 – Blogging

On my website, www.How2Become.com, I have a dedicated blog whereby members of my staff blog on a weekly basis. Blogging is highly-effective for driving traffic to your website or your Amazon sales-page. If you are going to blog, I recommend you use a WordPress website as it is great for this purpose. You should also ensure you blog on a regular basis. For example, it is far better to create a blog post every two weeks as opposed to doing ten blogs in one go and then not doing anymore for a six-month period. To gain traction from blogging, make sure you blog on a regular basis and create fantastic/lengthy content that is valuable to the reader. Finally, once you create your WordPress blog, be sure to add social media share buttons from the website **www.AddThis.com**.

#12 – Email signature

This is a fast and simple one to do – make sure you put a link to your book on Amazon in your email signature (and if you're a bestselling author, then make sure you mention that!).

#13 – Podcast interviews

Have a look around online for people who run podcasts in your niche/genre. For example, I have carried out a few podcast interviews for people who own self-publishing websites. This is a great, win-win situation for both you and the podcast owner. In addition to searching on Google for podcast websites, also try searching on iTunes.

#14 – Charity fundraising

Consider holding a charity fundraising event on a particular day. You could either:

- Hold a coffee morning and sell your books to everyone who attends. All the proceeds from books you sell at the coffee morning could go to charity;

Or

- Donate all proceeds from book sales on Amazon for one day.

Whilst the above two options won't make you any money, they will give you invaluable exposure for your book. Don't forget to tell the local press if you do hold a fundraising event or give away royalties to charity.

#15 – Get your book translated

To reach a wider audience, consider getting your book translated into different languages and then re-publish it on Amazon targeting different countries. To find a great translation outsourcer, head of to UpWork.com and search for a translator in your required language(s).

#16 – Goodreads.com

Sign up for the Goodreads author programme and create an event to promote your book launch party. To post an event on Goodreads, visit your profile settings and click on the "Edit My Author Profile" link on the top right. Once there, click the "events" link on the right side under your author picture, then click "add an event" in the upper right-hand corner of the screen. From there you can select the date, time, and venue for your event, as well as fill in additional details and invite your friends.

#17 - Enter awards

I have entered many awards during my time as an author and publisher and the publicity I have gained from them has been amazing. I always enter an award with the attitude - *I have nothing to lose by entering!*

As an author, there are many awards you can enter. Below are just a few of the many awards available for you to enter:

Don't forget, you have nothing to lose by entering the awards.

www.businessbookawards.co.uk

www.foyles.co.uk/Public/Biblio/Prizes.aspx

www.nationalbook.org

www.waterstones.com/book-awards

www.costa.co.uk/costa-book-awards/welcome

www.ipg.uk.com/awards

www.booktrust.org.uk/prizes

www.thebailliegiffordprize.co.uk

www.fcbg.org.uk

#18 - Building a list/database to promote your books and other products or services to

This must be one of the most powerful methods for growing your publishing business. Building a list means collecting people's names and email addresses so you can contact them at any time to offer them your latest books, training courses or products/services. At the time of writing, I have a list of over 100,000 previous customers. If you constantly try to 'build' your list, you will have a stream of new people to promote your books and products to.

There are many ways I build my list; however, the following method is the one that gives me most success. Within most my books I will offer my readers some types of useful bonus. For example, as part of this book I have created a free author toolkit that will help you get started on your writing and publishing journey at the website **www.AuthorToolkit.co.uk**. To access the toolkit, you need to enter your name and email address. You will notice I mention this toolkit right at the start of the book and at key stages throughout.

To build a list, you will need an appropriate service or piece of software, which enables you to capture people's names and email addresses on your website or landing page. There are many different types of services that will provide this, however I personally find that **www.MarketersChoice.co.uk** and **InfusionSoft.com** are exceptional marketing tools for this purpose. However, these tools are expensive and on that basis, I recommend you start off with **www.MailChimp.com**, or something similar.

You will also need something to offer people who opt-in to your list. The following list will give you some ideas as to the types of things you can offer your readers:

- Some form of downloadable 'toolkit' that helps the reader learn more about the information contained within your book;

- A free bonus chapter that is not contained within the book;

- A free online training video that helps your readers to accelerate their learning;

- The first chapter of your next book.

#19 - Newspaper and local media advertising

We are undoubtedly living in changing times, and fewer people are buying and reading newspapers, especially local ones! However, these can still be effective ways to test a book which you want to offer your customers. Here are a few important tips to consider when advertising in local or national printed newspapers:

- DO NOT pay the rate card price for the size advert you want. There are massive discounts to be had, especially a day or two before the paper goes to print. If there is advertising space left close to the print deadline, then you can get at least 50% off the rate card. When dealing with sales teams from local and national newspapers, be sure to barter hard on the price;

- Unless the price that you are paying for advertising space in local or national press is very cheap, you should always insist on your advert being placed on the right-hand page of the newspaper or magazine. Your advert will get more exposure on the right-hand side of a page, simply because the way that people read and scan newspapers naturally gravitates in that direction;

- When writing or creating your advert for the newspaper, I strongly recommend that you include a 'call to action'. A call to action is basically telling the reader of the advert to take some form of action, examples being:

  - Asking them to visit your website to download a FREE chapter of your new book.

  - Asking them to complete a form and send it back to you in exchange for some type of incentive.

  - Visit your website or business to get a discount, if they quote a specific reference name or number when buying your book.

#20 - Advertising using social media such as Facebook and Twitter

Social media advertising can be a very effective method to use for authors and self-publishers. Facebook, Twitter, Instagram and LinkedIn will allow you to pay for adverts that are placed right under the noses of your target audience. However, the difference between advertising on social media, as opposed to my preferred method of using pay-per-click advertising, is that people are not necessarily 'searching' for your product. This means that you must work harder to get a sale or conversion from social media advertising, whereas people searching via Google and other prominent search engines are more likely to be looking to buy your book or service.

The benefits of using Facebook, Instagram, Twitter, LinkedIn and other social media channels as an author and self-publisher are as follows:

- It is a free form of advertising if you choose not to pay for adverts.

- It allows you to build trust with your readers.

- It gives you the tools to promote new books and services.

- It allows you to build up a big following relatively quickly.

Whilst there are many benefits of using social media to generate leads and sales for your book writing and publishing business, there are pitfalls to be aware of too:

- It can be harder to generate sales via social media.

- If people are unhappy with your service, they have the option to tell everyone on Facebook. (Whilst this is a pitfall, it can work to your advantage, as it will force you to offer great products and customer service.)

- Once you start using social media, you MUST keep the pages and posts updated. If your page has been inactive for some time it can deter people from interacting with you or buying your book(s).

- There are many companies and websites out there offering you to 'buy' Facebook likes and Twitter followers. My advice is to avoid these at all costs. You should build your follows organically and by keeping your page engaging and interesting.

A great way to get more Facebook likes and Twitter followers is to create a competition on your page and Twitter feed. For example, let's assume you are going to be launching your new book in just 4 weeks' time, and you want to start creating a buzz around it. A great way to build 'likes' and followers is to offer people the chance to win a signed copy of your new book, if they like your Facebook page or follow you on Twitter. To get the most from this type of campaign, you should make a post on your page or feed and encourage people to 'share' the competition with their friends. I have known of some competitions going viral, so this is a great way to build a list of followers via social media for your business.

One final tip regarding social media posts and advertising is that video works much better than just text posts. If you head over to my Facebook page at **www.facebook.com/richardmcmunnauthor** you will notice that I create lots of free video content. Video content, in my experience, tends to get more engagement.

Oh, and by the way, make sure you mention your Facebook page at the start of your book and encourage your readers to connect with you there.

#21- Pay-per-click advertising

Pay-per-click advertising is great for promoting your business. The problem for many people who have no experience in using it is tackling the maze that is AdWords. If you get it wrong it will cost you dearly. Get it right, and it can work really well!

Pay-per-click (PPC) advertising was first introduced by Yahoo.com back in the early 2000's. It was an idea that would revolutionise advertising and the way that we use the Internet to search for the things that we want. Although Yahoo.com were the first 'smart cookies' to introduce PPC advertising, it was Google who really dominated the market by making their systems both highly effective and functional, but also relevant to what people were searching for – and this still stands true today.

'Relevance' is the key to PPC advertising, and Google certainly got this part right. The latest figures distributed reveal that over 70% of traffic searches are handled by Google. The remainder of traffic is spread about amongst the other search engine sites such as Bing, Ask and MSN. How the board members at Yahoo must now be kicking themselves for not dominating their own idea!

Anyway, what makes all this great for you as an author and publisher, is that you can get literally hundreds of 'relevant' visitors to your website within seconds. Of course, there are a number of pitfalls when using PPC advertising, but if you take the time to learn the system then you can generate a lot of sales in the process.

Earlier on I mentioned the word 'relevance'. Relevance is not only crucial to your advertising campaigns, it is also crucial to how many books you will sell from your website or blog at a profit. Here's why:

Keyword searches

People who search for goods or information online will type a word or a phrase into the search engine. Once they click 'search' they will be provided with hundreds, thousands, and sometimes millions of pages of 'relevant' websites. These websites are provided in order of most relevance, and Google will use its unique algorithm to achieve this. The websites that appear on the natural rankings of Google get most of the traffic for free, therefore there is a great incentive to get your website to appear on these free rankings. The only problem is that nobody, and I mean nobody, knows how Google's algorithm actually works, with the obvious exception of Google themselves.

Considering all the above information, it is vitally important that you choose your 'keywords and phrases' very carefully. In addition to the natural search rankings that Google creates, you will also notice that there are several 'sponsored results' at the very top of the page. These are what are called 'paid for advertising', or PPC as we better know them.

PPC does exactly what it says on the tin. Every time a person clicks on your advert, you have to pay for it, regardless of whether they buy anything or not! Therefore, there's a lot more to online advertising than simply getting traffic to your website, as there's also the art of conversion to consider too. In very basic terms, you will decide how much you are prepared to pay every time a person clicks through your advert. Because you are going to be selling a book, which may retail between £10 and £15, you will probably want to bid something like £0.10 - £0.20 per click.

Now here's the trick. In order to pay less for your adverts each time a person clicks through, you MUST make your advert **relevant** to what people are searching for. This can be achieved in a number of ways:

1. Choose a domain name that matches, or is similar to, the search term. These are more commonly referred to as Exact Matching Domains, or EMDs. Although EMDs are not beneficial to natural search engine rankings anymore, they can still work quite well for PPC advertising.

2. Make sure you include the search term in your advert – Google will make relevant domains and search terms bold so that they stand out.

3. Use 'capitalisation' in your adverts with the terms of Google's advertising policies. Again, these will allow the advert to stand out from the rest.

The more your advert stands out from the rest, the more people will click through on it. Because Google is so hell-bent on providing its users with **relevant** content, it will charge you less the more people who 'click through' on your advert (Click Through Rate - CTR). If more people are clicking through on your advert, then it must mean that your website is relevant to the search term! Bingo, everyone's a winner!

To help you get the most from PPC advertising, here are a few great tips:

- **Paying an outsourcer to set up your PPC campaign** – It is worth considering paying a professional outsourcer form Upwork.com to set up your campaign for you, if your budget will stretch this far. The reason for this is that you can end up wasting lots of money on clicks that will not convert, and a professional company will be able to test your adverts and keywords for you. Search Google for 'best pay per click advertising specialist upwork' and you will be presented with the best outsourcers to do the work for you.

- **Set your advertising budget low to begin with** – When you start advertising using PPC, I recommend that you set your daily budget quite low. This will allow you to test the market and see whether your book converts into a sale. If you are getting lots of visitors to your website, but none of them are buying or interacting, then there may be an issue with your website or sales-page.

- **Add negative keywords to your campaign** – Negative keywords can help you to reach the most interested customers, reduce your costs, and increase your return on investment (ROI). When you add negative keywords, your ad won't show to people searching for those terms or visiting sites that contain those terms. With negative keywords, you can:

  • Prevent your ad from appearing to people searching for or visiting websites about things that you don't offer;

  • Show your ads to people who are more likely to click them;

  • Reduce costs, by excluding keywords where you might be spending money but not getting a return;

  • When you select negative keywords, you'll want to choose search terms that are similar to your keywords, but signal that people are looking for a different product.

When you set up your Google AdWords account, Google will offer you a free telephone consultation to help you get started. Make sure you take up this free consultation.

#22 - Webinars

A webinar is an online event that is hosted by you as the author, and then broadcast to a select group of individuals through their computers via the Internet. A webinar is sometimes also referred to as a "webcast", "online event", or "web seminar".

A webinar allows you to share PowerPoint presentations, videos, web pages, or other multimedia content with your potential customers, who can be located anywhere.

Webinars typically have audio and visual components. The visual component of a webinar is shared through a web conferencing tool or Internet browser. The audio portion of a webinar is usually broadcast through the audience's computers (through speakers and media players) or through the telephone. Many authors are now using webinars as an effective way to provide details about their book(s) and how they will be of benefit to the reader. Of course, to hold a webinar, you will need a list of potential customers to present it to. This can be achieved by effective 'list-building', which I explained earlier. I usually run free webinars monthly, and it is not uncommon for me to sell upwards of 50 books per webinar that I run. There are several useful webinar software tools and platforms out there, including **www.GoToWebinar.co.uk** and **www.WebinarJam.com**.

#23 - YouTube

I have found YouTube to be one of the most beneficial ways to promote my books free of charge. There are literally no advertising costs associated with YouTube, and you can start getting traffic to your book or website fast. In fact, my YouTube channel (CareerVidz) has over 24,000 subscribers and has received in excess of 5,000,000 video views since launch. To put it into perspective, over 600,000 minutes of my video content is watched every month. That's a lot of free advertising for my books!

To make it easier for you to understand how you can generate free traffic and sales for your book, allow me to provide you with a step-by-step tutorial. This is the exact same tutorial I use time and time again to promote my books.

STEP 1 – Write and publish your book. Once you have published your book, you are now ready to start promoting it on YouTube.

STEP 2 – Open your YouTube account under your own author name, or alternatively with a name that is relevant to the genre or category your book falls under. For example, I decided to call my YouTube video account

'**CareerVidz**' as it is a channel that is predominantly aimed at the under 25 job-seekers market.

STEP 3 – Create a short 10-15 minute video that is relevant to your book, using **Camtasia Techsmith** or a similar software tool. If you are a MAC user, like me, you can use the inbuilt **QuickTime Player** to record your videos. The videos that I have created are presented on PowerPoint from my home computer. If you do not want to pay for the Camtasia Techsmith software, then you could simply use your iPhone or smartphone to record your video from home. For example, once I had published a book entitled *MECHANICAL COMPREHENSION TESTS*, I decided to create a short 12-minute video on this exact same subject. The video was educational and provided the viewer with important tips on how to prepare for this type of test. Here's the actual book that I published, to give you an idea what it looks like:

At the end of the video you should include one slide which directs people to either your website or Amazon, where they can buy your book.

STEP 4 – Once you have created and formatted your video, upload it to your YouTube channel. Make sure you title your video the same or similar to your book.

STEP 5 – Once you upload your video to your YouTube channel, you then have the option to edit your video in the 'VIDEO MANAGER' and add 'ANNOTATIONS'. Sporadically, I will add an annotation that encourages people to go to my website in order to download the book via the link, that I include within the 'DESCRIPTION of the YouTube video.

The annotation for this particular video will read:

"Download my book at the link below!"

The video description will say:

DOWNLOAD Richard's Book HERE: https://www.how2become.com/testing/mechanical-comprehension-tests/

You will note that I have included the full URL, including the extension 'https://' at the start of the link. If you do not include this, the link will not work.

Here's an image of the video on YouTube and what the annotation looks like:

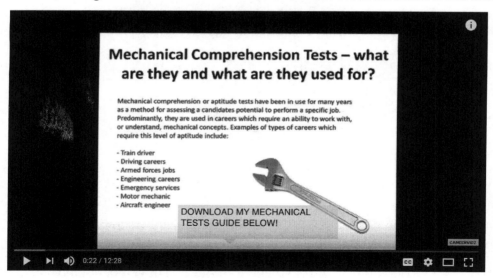

Mechanical Comprehension Test Questions and Answers - How To Pass Mechanical Aptitude Tests

431,381 views

You will notice the video above has received more than 430,000 views. That's a lot of free traffic for my book!

Tip: If you do not have a website yet to promote your book, simply add the URL to your book on Amazon.

Tips for getting the most from your YouTube channel

1. Your YouTube videos must offer high-quality and engaging content, as your viewers will have the opportunity to either give your video the 'thumbs-up' or the 'thumbs-down'. The more people who give it the thumbs-up, the more exposure YouTube will give your video in its ranking system. If lots of people give your video the thumbs' up, the video might eventually rank on Google for the exact phrase of your video title. To prove my point, my 'MECHANICAL COMPREHENSION TEST QUESTIONS AND ANSWERS' video ranks on the first page of Google – this is all free traffic for my book.

2. Because YouTube is owned by Google, it is in your interests to use this media channel to promote your book, simply because you can get lots of free traffic for your book.

3. Once your video has been live for a few months and is generating plenty of 'thumbs-up', consider 'monetising' your video. Monetising your videos essentially means an advertisement will be played at the start of your YouTube video. Each time the advertisement gets played in full, you will get paid a commission. There are certain criteria and rules that your video must meet before it can be eligible for monetisation, but it is something I strongly recommend you consider implementing.

4. You will have the opportunity to encourage people to 'subscribe' to your YouTube channel, too. At the time of writing, my CareerVidz YouTube channel has received over 5,000,000 video views and has more than 24,000 subscribers.

   Promoting my books on YouTube has proven to be a profitable way for me to sell my books to a wider audience, without the additional costs that can be involved with advertising.

5. To increase video views, pose a question during video and ask your viewers to place their answer in the comments section below the video on YouTube. You could ask your viewers for their opinion of a subject relevant to the video or you could ask them to tell you which video they want you to create for them next.

So, there you have it, 23 great ways to promote your book! Hopefully there are few there to help you get your book sales off the ground.

CHAPTER 22 –
Useful Links And Resources

USEFUL LINKS AND RESOURCES

Within this final chapter of the guide I have provided you with some links and resources which you may find useful.

MY VIP AUTHOR MENTORING PROGRAMME
www.RichardMentorMe.com

FREE AUTHOR TOOLKIT
www.AuthorToolkit.co.uk

FREE BOOK PROMOTIONAL WEBSITE
www.AboutTheAuthor.co.uk

ONLINE BOOK WRITING AND PUBLISHING TRAINING VIDEOS AND RESOURCES
www.BookCourse.co.uk

BOOK AWARDS
www.costa.co.uk/costa-book-awards/welcome/
www.ipg.uk.com/awards
www.booktrust.org.uk/prizes
www.businessbookawards.co.uk

HIGH-QUALITY BOOK COVER DESIGN
www.BookPublishingAcademy.com

PRINTING COMPANY
www.Bell-Bain.com

VIDEO CREATION SOFTWARE TOOL
www.techsmith.com/camtasia.html

ECOOMERCE SHOPPING CARTS AND EMAIL MARKETING SYSTEMS
www.marketerschoice.co.uk
www.infusionsoft.com
www.aweber.com
www.mailchimp.com

FREE WEBSITE BLOGS
www.blogger.com
www.weebly.com
www.wordpress.com

INDEPENDENT PUBLISHERS GUILD
www.ipg.uk.com

BOOK FAIRS
www.londonbookfair.co.uk
www.bookfairs.scholastic.co.uk
www.poetrybookfair.com

ISBN NUMBERS
www.nielsenisbnstore.com

BAR CODE GENERATOR SOFTWARE
www.nchsoftware.com/barcode

OUTSOURCING WEBSITES
www.UpWork.com
www.99Designs.com
www.Fiverr.com
www.PeoplePerHour.com

EBOOK CONVERSION FOR KINDLE
www.BookPublishingAcademy.com

PACKAGING WEBSITES
www.davpack.co.uk
www.viking-direct.co.uk

CHEAP DELIVERY COURIERS
www.parcelmonkey.co.uk

WEBINAR TOOLS
www.GoToWebinar.com
www.WebinarJam.com

NIELSEN BOOKDATA
www.nielsenbookdata.co.uk

BOOK DISTRIBUTORS
www.gardners.com
www.bertrams.com

BOOK PROMOTIONAL VIDEO CREATION SERVICE
www.fiverr.com/videosforall

RADIO STATIONS
www.hbauk.com/member-stations
www.radiomap.eu/uk

STOCK IMAGE WESBITES
www.bigstockphoto.com
www.istockphoto.com
www.shutterstock.com
www.fotolia.com

COPYRIGHT AND INTELLECTUAL PROPERTY INFORMATION
www.ipo.gov.uk
www.start.biz

BOOK REVIEW BLOGS
www.blog.feedspot.com/bookreview_blogs

LEAFLET/FLYER PRINTING AND ROLLER BANNER CREATION
www.print-junction.co.uk

PRESS RELEASE WEBSITE
www.uk.prweb.com

SECTION THREE –

My Life as an Award-Winning Published Author

I look back now and see leaving the Fire Service as a thoroughly liberating experience. I can remember walking on Whitstable beach with my dog the day I resigned and feeling like a free man. Whitstable is famous for its oysters and I looked around, took a deep breath of sea air and felt the world really *was* my oyster. I had no regrets at all and, best of all, now I could devote as many hours of the day as I wanted to progressing my business and publishing my books.

After the unsatisfactory experience I'd had trying to work with a traditional London publishing house I was very clear about how I wanted to grow my company. It was now time for me to put all my efforts into producing my own physical books, and doing it my way. I hadn't had the chance to learn half the mysteries of the publishing process I wanted to find out through working with a mainstream publisher, but did that put me off? Of course not!

Walking along the beach that day, I reached a groin and stepped up onto it, just as I'd done hundreds of times. I was excitedly thinking about my future plans when I jumped off the other side, down onto the pebbly beach. I don't think I realised the drop was quite as deep as it was, because I landed badly on my ankle and the result was I had to go to hospital. It turned out nothing was broken, but I did have to take it easy for a while as I recovered from the sprain.

In hindsight this was not an unhappy accident. I was forced to sit still and I used the time to think and plan and educate myself about how to publish books through Amazon. At the same time I began revising the copy I'd written for my eBooks, updating the content and generally improving and polishing it. I wanted my physical books to be the best quality possible, and to give my customers great value for money.

I realised that the cover of the books would need to be eye-catching, excellent quality and designed in such a way that they told the potential reader exactly what to expect from the book. With this in mind, I paid an expensive designer to create covers for me. I also recognised that getting the size of the book right was very important. This was something I hadn't had to consider when I was dealing with eBooks and CDs, and I didn't really know where to start.

As soon as I was back on my feet I took myself into a local Waterstones with a ruler and measured the dimensions of books in similar genres to mine. They were larger than regular fiction titles, but generally had fewer pages. From this basic research, I decided on page sizes and chose to aim for approximately 150-200 pages per book. If the content I already had would fill more than my targeted page count I decided I would put additional resources and bonus sections on the website, which would be a good way of attracting traffic and keeping in touch with customers.

More research told me that it would be wise to outsource certain skilled tasks I had no knowledge of, such as typesetting. I found this part of the journey really hard, which is why I wanted to share my experience and write this book you're reading now. I had no clue about so many things: ISBNs, BISAC Codes, spine widths and Kindle conversion, to name just a few. I was learning so much every day and it was time-consuming and often frustrating, as I had so little knowledge at the start. I never gave up and persevered, telling myself all the time, 'You only have to learn this once, and then you can repeat it a thousand times!'

Hopefully this book will make YOUR journey a lot smoother and easier, leaving you more time to concentrate on writing your book!

Once I'd cracked the process and worked out how to publish my books and sell them on Amazon I had new issues to contend with. Amazon Print-On-Demand was not yet in existence and I was exclusively using Amazon Advantage. This meant I had to store copies of my published books at home, package them and post them. As sales increased I eventually began running out of space, and so I rented an office in Kings Hill, West Malling. I wanted the labelling and packaging to look perfect and professional and so I decided to hire someone to help. Surprisingly, it was harder than you might think finding someone who could do this really well!

Eventually a young man called Joshua Brown applied for a packaging job. He was fresh out of university and had a degree in games design. I wasn't sure a temporary packing job was for him, but Josh was very enthusiastic and convinced me it was the perfect post for him at that time, even though his ambition was to eventually carve out a career as a games designer. I took Josh on for three hours a day, working as a packer and a general admin assistant, and things quickly grew from there. Josh was fascinated by the world of publishing and the online marketing work I was doing, and as time went on I started to trust him with more and more tasks. This was a real leap of faith for me as in the Fire Service I'd been used to being in control of absolutely everything, but happily it worked!

I decided to give Josh the chance of writing his own book so he could really learn the process from start to finish, and he jumped at the opportunity. *How to Become a Games Designer* went on sale on Amazon and became a bestseller. Now there was no stopping Josh! He was hooked on the business, and I made him Office Manager as we started to recruit researcher/writers and grow our catalogue.

Alongside this we started to create the YouTube channel, CareerVidz, as I discussed in Chapter 21 of SECTION TWO. From the YouTube CareerVidz channel we post a wide range of videos that are linked to our books, including general educational and job application tutorials right through to videos teaching you how to pass a Skype interview. The YouTube channel was extremely successful from the start. The first video I ever made was about how to pass a telephone interview. It was quite long and very basic, with just me talking over PowerPoint slides, but it started to get lots of views and today has been watched more than a million times!

By 2014 I'd written and published close to 150 physical books on Amazon and was running more and more training courses. I was developing courses to help coach other writers and authors and I was also providing a variety of author and publishing mentoring services, which is what I wanted to devote more of my time to. Josh was very willing to take on further responsibilities in the day-to-day running How2Become to allow me to concentrate on my mentoring and courses, but before I began to step away and give more tasks to Josh I had one big ambition I wanted to fulfil.

My goal was to WIN the Independent Publishers Guild (IPG) Awards. As I wrote in Chapter 11 of SECTION TWO, in 2012 and 2013 How2Become was shortlisted in the IPG's Publisher of the Year category as Best Newcomer, but that was not enough! You are only allowed to enter this newcomer category during your first three years of membership in the IPG, so 2014 was my last shot at finally winning that particular title.

I was full of optimism when I entered the awards, and once again How2Become was shortlisted. I desperately wanted to win, and on the night of the final I was very hopeful of victory. Unfortunately, when the winner was announced my heart sank. Despite my efforts, the 'best newcomer' was not How2Become. I was disappointed for the third time, but still determined to achieve my goal. Although this was the final year I could enter the Best Newcomer award, there were still other categories I could enter. I immediately set my sights on the 2015 awards, and straight away I began to think about what steps I could take to improve my chances of winning in another category the following year.

I looked around the room and spotted a lady called Sheila Bounford enthusiastically applauding the winners. It turned out Sheila was the former Executive Director of the IPG and now worked as a consultant. I immediately thought back to when I took part in the HSBC Start-Up Stars Awards in 2006, and how I asked Sally Preston of Babylicious for business advice, which proved very useful.

'I've got to talk to Sheila Bounford!' I thought, and later that evening I went over and introduced myself.

Sheila agreed to come and do some consultancy work at How2Become. I told her I was determined to win awards with the IPG and she took a good look at what I was doing with How2Become, visiting once a month for six months. Her expertise was invaluable. Sheila identified a number of areas for improvement. She said I needed to go to IPG events and start networking, and she told me I needed to invest in a new website and more SEO optimisation. In addition, I needed bigger premises and I had to hire more staff. 'At the moment, it's all about you, Richard, and you've run it as far as you can,' Sheila told me. I listened and I knew Sheila was right. After writing so many books I was in danger of burning out, and I definitely needed more staff. It was time for me to seriously step aside but, as I've already said, I wasn't going anywhere until I'd won an award!

Josh and I implicated all the changes Sheila recommended and we hired more staff, building a brilliant team around us. Josh was picky and very patient in the recruitment process. He only took on writers and other staff he believed would not just do the job to a very high standard, but also fit in well with the rest of the office. I saw how Josh's patience paid off, and today we not only have a fantastic team of creatives working at How2Become, but there is also a great vibe and a very relaxed atmosphere in the office.

In 2015, we put in for the IPG Specialist Consumer Publisher of the Year and the Nielson Digital Marketing Award. How2Become was shortlisted in both categories. The competition was tougher for us now in some ways, as we were no longer in the newcomer category, and guess what? Once again, we didn't win! It was disappointing but I was determined to carry on and achieve my dream. How2Become had its most profitable year and I was hopeful that NEXT year was going to be the year we finally got our hands on a trophy! In my mind, perseverance and determination ALWAYS win.

As it happened, when the 2016 awards came around and we were shortlisted for the same two categories again, I didn't actually care if we won or not. That may surprise you, given my history of striving to succeed, but by then I was so proud of what I'd already achieved that I really was not that bothered. How2Become was in fantastic shape. I'd made more than £5 million from my business at the time, and I had such a great team working for me.

I took the whole office to the award ceremony. I was determined not to get my hopes up and told everyone I didn't expect to win, which was true. I was simply looking forward to a good night out, celebrating our achievements together and being proud to be shortlisted. Then, of course, the unexpected happened. It was a bit like going into your driving test and expecting to fail, then breezing through and getting a surprise pass!

We won not one, but BOTH categories. This was the pinnacle of my publishing career and I was absolutely ecstatic. How2Become was the IPG's Specialist Consumer Publisher of the Year and we also bagged the Nielson Digital Marketing Award! This was the icing on the cake for me.

I gave several interviews afterwards, including one to the Lancashire Evening Post. The paper ran a story under the headline 'Blaze of glory for firemen turned writer'. They also printed a picture me holding the two awards, looking ridiculously pleased!

The Evening Post had followed my story for a few years, after I donated 150 books to a new library at my old school, Balshaw's High School in Leyland. When Balshaw's heard about my success with How2Become they asked if they could add me to their 'Hall of Fame'. I was absolutely delighted to tell them that yes, of course they could! Who would have thought that a former pupil who left with three GCSEs would join the prestigious list of former pupils now feted as 'The Pride of Balshaw's'? To be recognised in this way, alongside people like Manchester United footballer Phil Jones and the former Chief Constable of Merseyside Police, Sir James Sharples, is an incredible honour, and something I'm immensely proud of. I cast my mind back now to the day I opened my GCSE results and thought to myself, *What am I going to do now?* The fact I feature on my school's Hall of Fame just goes to show you CAN achieve whatever you want in life, if you're prepared to work hard, persevere and never give in!

In 2107 How2Become once again won two awards, including the IPG Nielson Digital Marketing Award for the second year running. This is what was said on the night:

How2Become secures this Award for a second successive year, having impressed again in 2016 with campaigns including YouTube videos and a new 'customer funnelling' strategy. It led to a steep rise in sales, more than half of which were made direct to consumers from its website.

"A lot of big corporates could learn from how it segments audiences and uses non-traditional channels," judges said."For a company of its size the marketing is a massive achievement."

I'm very happy to say that our other award was for Josh, who was named Young Independent Publisher of the Year. That really was the cherry on the cake! Josh had gone through such a rapid development with my guidance and he thoroughly deserved this victory. He'd been working as Operations Director for more than a year, and since then I've appointed him as Managing Director. I did this because I knew it was FINALLY time for me to step aside from How2Become and focus on my passion for mentoring other authors. That is how I've come to publish this book you are reading now, and to tell you about my personal journey, because I hope it will inspire and encourage YOU to get your own book published.

I'm delighted to be able to devote many more hours to coaching other writers. I love what I do. I get to meet amazing people and hear incredible stories about their challenges, tragedies and triumphs. I thoroughly enjoy helping other writers navigate all the various stepping stones on their journey to becoming a published author, and it's a pleasure to share my knowledge and expertise and see other people benefit and grow as writers and publishers.

When authors I've mentored get great reviews or see their book become bestsellers on Amazon, I could not be happier. It's a great feeling and extremely satisfying. The same goes for when I receive reviews for my own books, and any of the How2Become titles, from readers telling me they have achieved success in getting the job they always wanted. How2Become has helped thousands of people find employment in a variety of jobs, and that is extremely rewarding.

LESSONS LEARNED FROM BEING AN AWARD-WINNING PUBLISHED AUTHOR

Be calm. I've learned to be a calmer person and take my time when making decisions. In the Fire Service, I had to take decisions very quickly but in business it is rarely necessary. Take your time and make the right decision. It will be worth it.

Be a nice person. Even when I feel incredibly driven and determined to succeed I avoid being ruthless and always stay respectful to other people. Be kind to all the people you deal with when you grow your business – it's the decent thing to do, and you might need them again at some point in the future!

Be a motivator. I learned in the Fire Service how to manage staff and get the best out of them. As soon as a member of staff feels undervalued or demotivated they are no use to you. It is your job to motivate your staff and make them feel valued. If you are not running a business I would apply this lesson to the relationships you have with outsourcers. Treat them well and you and your books will benefit.

Keep yourself motivated. I know that if I stay creative, I will always be happy. I love coaching people and helping them take their books to market. I also like to start new businesses. I recently set up an art business by selling canvas prints through KingsHillArt.com. Feed your creativity as much as you can - it will keep you motivated and make you not just a happier author, but a happier person.

Spend time with your family and relax. In the early days of my author/ publishing career I didn't spend enough time with my family and I was terrible in relationships because I was working 18 hours a day. Now I have learned there is no point in working hard and earning great money if you are not enjoying your freedom. Take time out and spend it with the people who matter.

Money does not buy you happiness. I enjoy the financial freedom being an author brings me, but I know money is not the key to happiness. Fulfilling my creativity and helping others makes me happy. Recognise what makes you happy and DO IT!

Closing thoughts for YOUR successful future

I hope I have not come across as someone who is bragging about their success, because that is not my intention at all. I feel that my story just shows how far you can go, if you put your mind to it. I started out in my cellar, writing books on an old computer, and I've now reached a point where I can say that my company is hugely influential in the industry. As long as you are willing to work hard, the sky is the limit.

I hope you have found this book to be informative, helpful, and above all inspiring. I'd like to end by sharing something I've observed with interest over the years. Below are four key character traits of successful people:

1. They believe in themselves - The first factor in being a successful as an author and publisher is self-belief. Regardless of what anyone tells you, you *can* do it. Just like anything in life, you have to be prepared to work hard in order to be successful. Make sure you have the self-belief. Fill your mind with positive thoughts, and always ignore the doubters. Surround yourself with like-minded, positive entrepreneurs and don't spend time with negative people.

2. They choose to be successful - The second factor is choice. During my career I have been amazed at how many people have said to me: 'You are so lucky to have the life you do.' My success is not down to luck, it is down to choice. I choose to work hard, and I want you to do the same, too.

3. They persevere - Perseverance is my favourite word. Everybody comes across obstacles or setbacks in their life, but it is what you do about the setbacks that is important. View every setback as an opportunity; an opportunity for improvement and an opportunity to learn.

4. They have a mentor to guide and coach them - Successful people will always have a mentor. That mentor will be instrumental in their success, and will be the one person who helps them to achieve the success they deserve.

To your success,

Richard McMunn

Richard McMunn

If you would like me to personally mentor you to write your first book, please visit:

www.RichardMentorMe.com

For book writing and publishing training courses please go to:

www.BookPublishingCourses.com